sister
STRONG

sister
STRONG

{ *Living in Harmony with the Women in Our Lives* }

HAILEY & MANDI GARDINER

CFI

An imprint of Cedar Fort, Inc.
Springville, Utah

ISBN 13: 978-1-4621-2323-0

Published by CFI, an imprint of Cedar Fort, Inc.
2373 W. 700 S., Springville, UT 84663
Distributed by Cedar Fort, Inc., www.cedarfort.com

Library of Congress Cataloging-in-Publication Data on file.

Cover design by Shawnda T. Craig
Cover design © 2019 Cedar Fort, Inc.
Edited by Misty Moncur and Allie Bowen
Typeset by Kaitlin Barwick

Printed in Canada

10 9 8 7 6 5 4 3 2 1

Printed on acid-free paper

To Linda

We love you and miss you!

Contents

Introduction: Becoming Sister Strong 1

Chapter 1: Living in Harmony 9

Chapter 2: Remembering Who You Are 14

Chapter 3: Celebrating Differences 25

Chapter 4: Like Mother, like Daughter 36

Chapter 5: Finding Your Tribe 48

Chapter 6: Laughing It Off 55

Chapter 7: Friendship 64

Chapter 8: Being a Peacemaker 78

Chapter 9: Maybe It's Me 88

Chapter 10: Being the Only One 95

Chapter 11: Seeing with Our Hearts 109

Chapter 12: Making It Count, Making It Kind 117

Chapter 13: Forgiveness 132

Chapter 14: Loving Our Neighbor 144

Chapter 15: Hope in Christ 154

Acknowledgments 159

About the Authors 163

Introduction

BECOMING
SISTER STRONG

{ Hailey }

Mandi and I come from a large family of six girls and two boys. Our family life together has certainly been a wild ride! I always say that I was an only child for a short year and a half before our second sister, Allie, was born. Mandi came into the picture eighteen months later. The three of us were so close in age that we were often dressed up in matching outfits, complete with those fabulously '90s oversized bows topping our heads.

Our sister Lindsay was born four years after Mandi, and then over the next eight years, our sister Abby, our brothers, Ben and Tim, and our baby sister Lucy joined the family, bringing the total to ten. Have you ever seen the movie *Cheaper by the Dozen*? Remember that scene where the frog escapes in the kitchen right when everyone's making their lunches for school and lands right in the scrambled eggs, splattering them all over the family sitting at the breakfast table? That's pretty much what every day in our house growing up was like. A little bit of chaos mixed with a whole lot of food and fun!

Anyone who has grown up in a large family will probably relate to what we call BFP, or "big family problems."

Our mom always cooked enough food to feed an army, but as our appetites increased, we'd be on the edge of our seats waiting for the blessing on the food to be finished. As soon as we said "amen," everyone would go into survival mode and load up their plates a mile high, knowing there was a slim chance of getting a second helping of Mom's buttery mashed potatoes once all ten people had taken their share.

Our family grew to eventually include "The Kahuna," our fifteen-passenger van that carted us (as well as our friends) to school, church, all our sports and activities, and even across the country on our family road trips.

Our large family attracts the stares of strangers every time we go out together. Especially at restaurants and on airplanes, where Dad says you can see the fear shining in people's eyes and can almost hear them saying, "Please, PLEASE don't sit next to me."

On Sunday mornings if we weren't up at the crack of dawn before everyone else, we'd be shivering under a cold shower. It would take us about an hour to get everyone looking somewhat presentable with both shoes on their feet and in the car to get to church, or anywhere else for that matter. Once we made our grand (and by "grand" I mean *at least* fifteen-minute-late) entrance into church, the whole congregation would watch us file in and take our seats because our family alone took up an *entire* pew.

There are so many of us that if we didn't do a head count before leaving to go anywhere, someone (usually Lindsay—the quiet one) was bound to be left behind.

We almost always shared bedrooms. When our family was temporarily renting a small townhome several years ago, all six of us girls had to share one bedroom, one closet, and one bathroom. Six girls, one bathroom, my friends. That was an adventure.

Our Mom grew up in a really musical family and brought her musical gifts and love for performing into our home. If there is a microphone available, it's only a matter of time before Grandpa or one of our uncles steps up and gets the show on the road. They never miss an opportunity to entertain and fill a room with music!

Though we all grew up taking piano lessons, playing violin and cello in our middle school orchestras, and performing in choirs, dance recitals, and show groups from the time we could talk, it wasn't until Mom taught Mandi, Allie, and me a church hymn in three-part harmony that we discovered our natural ability to harmonize. She was blown away by how quickly we picked up our parts and how easily we were able to sing them at such a young age. We started performing at church, in our community, at retirement homes, in restaurants—anywhere Mom could get us in. She would teach us new songs, slowly picking out our individual parts on the piano and having us practice together daily, despite our constant complaining and protesting.

Because we've been harmonizing and singing together forever, it's become second nature to us, something we don't even have to think about. Before we learned how to play songs other than "Mary Had a Little Lamb" on our instruments, we sang almost all our music a cappella. We'd create our own complex arrangements in three-part harmony and would snap or clap out the tempo as we sang to keep us on the beat. Being able to sing a cappella allowed us to perform anywhere without accompaniment, which basically meant Mom could ask us to sing "Happy Birthday" or "Have Yourself a Merry Little Christmas" to anyone and everyone: the cashier at the grocery store, our waitress, or a neighbor who had stopped by. You name a place, and we've probably been asked to sing there.

As we gained experience performing together in church and in our community, our parents encouraged us to start entering local talent competitions. We sang "Somewhere Over the Rainbow" in the Mt. Pleasant's Got Talent Fourth of July competition and ended up winning! We used our earnings to record our first EP of a few hymns and classic songs in a local studio. Though we'd recorded background vocals on family members' projects before, our first experience recording our own music together felt totally different. We knew we had something special going, and from then on, we were hooked.

As young teens, we'd spend hours listening to our Radio Disney CDs on our Walkmans, dreaming of singing with the Jonas Brothers, touring the world, and having our own show on the Disney Channel. Our parents decided that moving to Los Angeles could provide us with more opportunities to pursue our young dreams, so they packed up our family of ten and drove the Kahuna across the country to California.

After a few months of meetings, auditions, and recording sessions, we learned that things weren't going to just magically work out for us the way we'd hoped. We also learned that handing things over to important and connected (a.k.a. name-dropping) industry executives who oversold on their promises resulted in a whole lot of disappointment and rejection.

We worked with vocal coaches, songwriters, stylists, publicists, choreographers, and producers who promised to make us the next big thing and tried to tell us what our sound should be and what we should look like. A pop label told us we needed to go country because we weren't edgy enough to be pop. A team of "top" songwriters from across the country wrote cheesy songs for us, one of which included the *ridiculous* lyric "Let me see you dance like you've got ants in your pants." We thought it was hilarious when we listened to the demos, but we realized that if we wanted to stay true to ourselves, we couldn't count on anybody else to create music for us. We each started learning how to play the guitar and piano so we could write our own songs.

My sisters and I worked with choreographers who'd toured with the biggest celebrities to craft cute dances to each of our numbers that ended up making us look like we were trying *way* too hard. It was all a little too peppy for our laid-back style. Needless to say, we never performed any of the songs other people wrote for us or busted out a single one of those dances on stage.

Stylists made us up in over-the-top clothes, makeup, and hairstyles and told us that we needed to start getting our eyebrows done and that we should use shapewear under our clothes to smooth out and slim down our growing teenage bodies.

We were invited to audition for several popular talent competition TV shows, and always made it through the first few rounds, usually just before the televised episodes, before the casting directors would call us and deliver the news that we'd been cut. As our family learned to handle rejection and say no to those things that didn't feel right or didn't align with our values, our vision of who we really wanted to be as artists and as people slowly came into focus. Looking back, we were put in front of a lot of powerful and connected people, but God had a different plan that allowed us to stay true to our faith and grounded as a family.

During our time in California, we were encouraged to start a YouTube channel for interested labels, managers, and executives to view our work. We had already been making crazy family videos over the years that we thought were pretty funny and made our parents laugh, so we started tracking the charts and learning popular songs, posting videos of us singing them live to our channel.

We welcomed the online world into our home, sharing sister moments, shenanigans, and our signature blooper reel in our videos. Though we initially felt discouraged when our efforts over several years didn't result in a record deal or the traditional path of success in the music industry, we learned that rejection is often God's protection. Having complete control over every step of creating our content turned out to be the greatest blessing and allowed us to develop as arrangers, instrumentalists, songwriters, and producers.

Slowly and steadily, as people from all over the world discovered and listened to our music on YouTube and Spotify, we built an independent online following that has allowed us to be true to ourselves and to create beautiful things together as sisters. We've recorded and released lots of songs together, filmed and edited many music videos, and gained valuable live performance experience by going on tour as the headliners as well as openers for other artists.

As Lindsay, Abby, and Lucy got older, they discovered their own musical talents and have been included as members of Gardiner Sisters more recently. I'm not sure that any of the most valuable experiences we have shared together would have happened if we'd gotten signed, won a singing competition on TV, or gone on tour with the most popular act in the world at that time.

{ Mandi }

As our music evolved and our career path changed, our sisterhood and goals shifted along with it. We found our vibe and learned how to lock in harmonies so we could enter the studio or walk on stage and perform like it was second nature to us. Though our music creation began to flow effortlessly, our sisterhood and relationships with other women around us could not be navigated so easily. Oftentimes we struggled to write together, be creative together, and at times even speak kindly to one another. Our work became difficult to maintain because our sister harmony, both literally and figuratively, was off-pitch.

All three of us—Hailey, Allie, and I—reached a point where we knew we had to put our sister relationships first in order to restore our strong family bond. We began journeys of self-discovery. In our time spent on better understanding who we were as individuals and how the Lord sees us, we learned some valuable insights about how to be better sisters to each other. In this book, we hope some of our findings are helpful to you as you navigate family relationships and harmonious living with the people you love most and come to interact with on your journey of life.

Knowing how many women feel, especially in regards to themselves, we hope *Sister Strong* will ease the pressure you may feel to be perfect and help you put your time and energy into relationships that add happiness and meaning to your life. We hope that sharing our personal stories and hard lessons learned will help you realize how similar we are to you and how our individual stories can make us stronger together when we share them. This book is meant to show you how normal our family interactions are, as we work every day to better love and understand each other—regardless of how our family may come across on the internet. We wanted to be raw and realistic, so you could feel you're not alone in family struggles, personality differences with others, and hard times.

Our greatest hope is that this book will help turn you to your Savior, Jesus Christ, to try and live like Him, loving the way He loves. Making Christ the center of your life and putting Him at the head of all of your relationships will help you grow closer to Him and to family, friends, and strangers alike. Following

His example and implementing His character into your own personality and actions will change your life for the better. As we have learned together as sisters, when Christ is involved in your relationships, you will not fail. He is the tie to strong bonds and unity with others. He has the power to make us sister strong and make our relationships unbreakable.

We want each of you to feel our love, for we too love you like family and care about you with all the sisterly love we have! Life can be full of difficult times and rough turns, but you will never be alone in the struggle. We hope *Sister Strong* will inspire you to bond with women you look up to and help you have the courage you need to reevaluate and improve current relationships in your life.

Though our music career has evolved and changed, we have learned through the ups and downs of sisterhood how to prioritize those things that matter most. We have accepted that not every day is a harmonious day, and relationships take time and effort to write that perfect melody together.

We hope you enjoy learning more about our family—the struggles and the hard times and all the good that has made us stronger as siblings. We hope you feel inspired to dig deeper in your interactions with others and in the way you see the women in your life. Thank you for letting us share some of our story and for letting us be real with you. We're truly all in this together, and we love and acknowledge each of you. Thank you for inspiring us by the way you live and for showing us what it means to be sister strong.

Chapter 1

LIVING IN HARMONY

{ Hailey }

One of the questions we get asked most often is "How do you get along with each other so well?" The short answer is, we don't. At least, not all the time. Our relationships as sisters and as members of a performing group together have always been intertwined and sometimes hard to separate. We were (and still are) a semi-normal, albeit large and crazy, family with imperfect relationships. What you see in our videos and interactions online are just moments, little glimpses into our sisterhood. While we strive to be positive and to create encouraging and uplifting content, we're often only showing you one small aspect of our family dynamics.

Like most siblings, we do sometimes struggle to get along with each other. It became challenging to find balance between our working and personal relationships with each other and to keep things fun as we grew older and our differences and desires became more distinct. Harmonizing together may come naturally to us as sisters, but our ability to walk in harmony with each other doesn't always come as easily.

Allie and Abby, bless them, have the great "gift" of being able to sing convincingly off-key, on purpose. One of them will start singing and everyone joins in with their own "harmony part," creating a real disastrous mess. It makes us laugh until we cry when we sound that awful together, and we couldn't be more proud of our younger siblings who have carried on the tradition.

The discord we create when all of us are singing off-key is similar to what it's like to live in disharmony with each other. When we allow contention and discord in our relationships, it's like trying to sing together without paying attention to the structure and arrangement of the song entirely. We may be members of the same family, with shared physical traits, similar senses of humor, and love for music, but as individuals we are all very different from each other.

So how do we do it? How do we live and work together and love each other when we experience the disharmony that naturally results as we make mistakes, experience hardships and heartbreak, and feel separation growing between us? The truth is that we don't have it all figured out, but we are constantly learning as we go, making adjustments in our lives to allow space for each of us to flourish.

Picture this. You and your friends decide to come out to one of our concerts and, after finding your seat, pulling out your snacks, and getting comfortable, wait in anticipation for the show to start. When the big moment comes and the curtain rolls up, we'd walk out on stage and the crowd would go wild. But then each of us would pick a random starting note and proceed to rock out to our first song together. It wouldn't matter if we nailed the lyrics, stayed on tempo, and sang our harmony parts correctly in their respective keys because together we'd sound awful!

What if, instead, one of us pulled out a pitch pipe, played a chord on guitar, or softly played our starting note on the piano so we would all know where to begin? Starting on the correct note would allow us to find our individual harmonies and sing our song together in the right key. Our harmonies would weave in and out of each other, occasionally landing on the same notes as one another, and the song would still flow beautifully even though each of us would be singing a different part.

Just like we'd need to hear our starting note to center ourselves before singing a song a cappella, when our lives are centered on Jesus Christ, He makes it possible for us to live in harmony with each other.

Each of us stands under those same bright lights shining down on the stage of life. Though we may be singing different harmony parts, we're all still part of the same song.

As daughters of God, we're all a part of His family choir. Each of us sings in our own one-of-a-kind, recognizable voice, offering differences in tone, phrasing, and approach from the other women around us. He doesn't compare us to each other or think that some of us are better than others. Every voice matters to Him. Our unique voices combine in harmony to create something beautiful, complex, and unified when we're centered on Jesus Christ and His gospel.

Living in harmony is about showing up and doing your part, even when you feel like it might not make a huge difference. I've avoided singing in the church choir for years, probably because I felt like I'd paid my dues by singing at baptisms, sacrament meetings, and funerals throughout our childhood. So when my friend Gill recently asked me to sing in the ward choir, my initial reaction was to say, "I'll pass." But because I love her (and because she promised me cupcakes—she knows the way to my heart), I decided to do it.

When it came time for us to sing a hymn in a church meeting, I found myself unexpectedly enjoying it. I felt like a happy fool standing up there as a member of that choir, and I couldn't stop smiling! I'd been going solo and taking myself so seriously as an "artist" for so many years that I'd forgotten how singing in a choir can actually be really fun!

I'd also forgotten what it felt like to be surrounded by lots of other women in a choir who are singing every word to the song along with you. Your voice almost disappears as it blends in with the sound of the voices surrounding you, and after a while it feels like you're all singing with just one voice. Though my voice may be small, the sound of our little ward choir just wouldn't be the same without it. The same goes for every other woman who decides to get up on the stand, pick up the sheet music, and add her voice to the choir.

In our family, we've found that as we draw closer to and strive to become more like our Savior, Jesus Christ, He helps us draw closer to each other. He gives each of us the courage to sing our own lines with confidence. He multiplies our strengths. Sometimes, if we start getting too comfortable, He rewrites our parts to challenge and refine us and make us better singers. He makes it possible for us to reach even those notes we think are out of our range.

We try to cheer each other on when it's someone's turn to solo, letting each sister have her moment to shine in the spotlight. We step out in life together, centered on Christ, who then blends our differences into gorgeous harmony.

This is sisterhood. This is what it means to be sister strong.

Being sister strong is not about losing yourself in the role of a sister, daughter, mother, wife, friend, roommate, aunt, or cousin, or letting other women in your life run the show for you. It's about taking responsibility for the quality of the relationships in your life. It's about showing up exactly as you are and joining hands with your sisters, who are singing their hearts out, loving them regardless of whether they have perfect pitch.

When we allow Christ to be our unifier, we can live in harmony even with those who couldn't be more different from ourselves, or those who may have hurt us and are hard to love. And sisters, it starts with you and me. It starts in our homes, our neighborhoods, our classrooms, and our churches. You better believe I'm showing up and adding my voice to this choir, so won't you come and sing with us?

In this book, we'll invite you to take a look at your relationships with the women in your lives. The principles and stories that we're sharing are true, some humorous and light and some a little more on the serious side. We're letting you in on some of the most valuable lessons we've learned about sisterhood. We may not be relationship experts, but we've learned a thing or two as we've put these principles into practice.

The best way to live in harmony with the women in our lives is to center ourselves on Jesus Christ. He can unite us, heal us, and help us to forgive, set boundaries, shift our perspectives, and increase our capacity to love. He can walk with us no matter what stage of life we may be in, or what state our relationships may be in. Whether we're sixteen or ninety-six, we can partner with Him to find lasting peace and happiness in our relationships. But don't just take our word for it; we encourage you to try it out for yourselves!

I believe that when you choose to prioritize your relationship with God and allow Him to work with your heart, He will increase your capacity to love and improve every other relationship in your life.

Sister, we need each other! Let's lock arms and start loving each other a little better. Let's become sister strong together.

Chapter 2

REMEMBERING WHO YOU ARE

{ Hailey }

Sisters, we are living in a time of crisis. I'm not just referring to craziness that we hear about every day on the news. I'm talking about a crisis of identity. There has never been a time in the history of this world that the adversary has worked harder to get us to forget who we truly are. Satan is waging a war on our souls more fiercely than ever before. He targets all of God's children, trying to drag us down into his trap of misery by telling us lies about our worth, purpose, and abilities. His most dangerous and effective tactic is to "destroy our belief in and knowledge of our relationship with God."[1]

Many of us are going through a divine identity crisis.

We as women have to engage in this battle every day, often feeling anxious, depressed, inadequate, and unsure of who we are and who we want to be. We're bombarded with voices everywhere that tell us we will never be enough.

The adversary is in constant competition with God for our souls. God wants to exalt you, love you, and bless you. Satan wants to ruin you and make you miserable like he is. You cannot let him. You have to fight back! Your greatest weapon against him is the knowledge you have that you are a child of God. You need to know that who you are is, always has been, and always will be enough for Him.

From the ages of twelve to eighteen, all the girls in our family participated in Young Women. Every Sunday we'd all stand up together and recite the Young Women theme. This theme begins with a statement that we still have memorized, one that I wish all of you could stand with us and say out loud: "We are daughters of our Heavenly Father, who loves us, and we love Him."[2]

Boyd K. Packer taught this truth beautifully: "You are a child of God. He is the father of your spirit. Spiritually you are of noble birth, the offspring of the King of Heaven. Fix that truth in your mind and hold to it. However many generations in your mortal ancestry, no matter what race or people you represent, the pedigree of your spirit can be written on a single line. You are a child of God!"[3]

Sisters, remember who you are! You are a daughter of the God of the universe. He created you. He is your Heavenly Father, and you are His child. He loves you unconditionally. Let this knowledge anchor you to Him. We are part of His mighty kingdom, each of us of noble birth. Nothing anyone ever says about me, or you, can change our divine identity and destiny.

Knowing that we are all daughters of God binds us to each other and makes it possible for us to live in harmony.

One of Satan's favorite tactics is to get us to compare ourselves to each other. When we remember who we are, we don't have to weigh ourselves against others to discover how much we are worth. God makes room for all of us to stand tall and sing out.

Remembering who we are also allows us to walk through the challenges of life with a quiet confidence, without trying to look like our lives are perfect or that we've always got it all together. Girl, no matter what things look like on the outside, ain't NOBODY got it all together. We're all imperfect. Heaven knows we all struggle. We might not struggle with the same things as our neighbor, friend, cousin, or sister, but we can strengthen and empathize with each other in ways that no one else can.

One Sunday, I shared some of my personal struggles with anxiety in a church meeting. I was a hot mess, y'all. I was yanking tissues out of that box on the pulpit like nobody's business. After the meeting, another woman I didn't know well stopped me in the hallway and said, "You are so beautiful. You have the light of Christ in you."

She was able to see past my puffy eyes, streaked makeup, and self-doubts and could see the light and the good in me. I felt so grateful to feel understood and seen for who I truly was in that moment! I believe that her ability to selflessly extend a genuine compliment, friendship, and kindness toward me was a sign of her own inner confidence.

Do you think that a woman who constantly tears herself down, beats herself up, and needlessly compares herself to other people is going to have the capacity to love her sister in *her* time of need? It may be possible, but I'm pretty sure that it comes much more naturally to a woman who is grounded in her own identity and knows her own infinite worth as a daughter of God.

Nothing can unify us more as sisters than the love of God can. Only when our own hearts are anchored and filled with God's love can that love then overflow to others. This applies not only to the relationships we have with other women but also to our dating and marriage relationships.

When I first started dating my husband, Cayden, I knew immediately that I wanted to marry him. He was full of light and confidence. He was deeply kind and bright. His sense of identity was evident in the way he carried himself and treated others, and that, to me, was what made him so attractive. It certainly didn't hurt that he was also the most handsome man I'd ever set my two little eyes upon. I looked like a smiling fool every time I was around him, and I felt lifted and good when I was in his presence. I had never felt that kind of automatic respect and admiration for anyone before, and I knew that he was someone I would always look up to.

Cayden knew who he truly was. He knew that he was a son of God, and his steadiness in his own divine identity allowed him to treat me as a daughter of God.

Before he came to pick me up for our first date, I started to get really nervous. Thoughts of uncertainty began filling my mind. I had been so impressed with Cayden during the time we'd spent together as friends and started to feel like little imperfect me wouldn't be enough for us to be anything more than that. While I put my makeup on and did my hair, I pulled out my phone and started listening to a talk by Elaine S. Dalton called "Remember Who You Are!"

From the moment I pressed play, I felt like she was standing right in front of me, giving me a much-needed pep talk.

"Each of you has inherited a royal birthright," she says. "Each of you has a divine heritage. 'You are literally the royal daughters of our Father in Heaven.' Each of you was born to be a queen."[4]

Her words gave me such a confidence boost that I remember looking at myself in the mirror when I'd finished putting on my makeup and seeing someone almost unrecognizable. I couldn't give the credit to any of the makeup I had put on my face. Whoever was looking back at me certainly *looked* like a queen! I felt confident, assured, and beautiful, and I seemed to be glowing from the inside out.

Our first date was just as wonderful as I'd hoped it would be, as well as our subsequent path to marriage, because I made the effort to remember my divine worth and was filled with reassurance from my Heavenly Father that I had every reason to be confident. Imagine if I had given in to my doubts and insecurities or allowed myself to feel awkward or unworthy and cancelled our date! I would have missed out on the greatest blessing I have in my life.

Though we are imperfect and we disagree, just like every other married couple, Cayden and I are able to love each other best when we are first anchored in our individual relationships with God. The love we feel for Him and from Him overflows into our marriage. I have seen this same principle apply to all other relationships in my life, including those with my mother, sisters, in-laws, grandmothers, and girl friends. The more anchored we are in Christ, the more easily we're able to love and accept others just as they are. God can then use us to accomplish His purposes, to serve and love others despite our differences.

We literally shine when we know and carry the truth in our hearts that we are daughters of God. On our first date, I knew that because Cayden was grounded in his identity as a son of God, he would be able to see that same light within me. Light attracts light, but he was only able to see it when I had the inner confidence to let it shine.

So get your shine on, sisters! The world needs YOU, exactly as you are, shining brightly in your divine truth!

Women who remember their divine identity are naturally going to stand out and be different. We can't be women who are "content to fit in," as Elaine Dalton says. We must have the courage to stand out. When we let our light shine, other women will see it, worthy men will see it, and we will be able to shine truth on the lies of the world about who we are and what we can do.

Since my first date with my husband, I've gone back and listened to Sister Dalton's talk many times. I love her take on what she called "deep beauty," which is "the kind of beauty that shines from the *inside* out." She continued:

> It is *spiritual* attractiveness. Deep beauty springs from virtue. It is the beauty of being chaste and morally clean. It is the kind of beauty that you see in the eyes of virtuous women like your mother and grandmother. It is a beauty that is earned through faith, repentance, and honoring covenants.
>
> The world places so much emphasis on physical attractiveness and would have you believe that you are to look like the elusive model on the cover of a magazine. The Lord would tell you that you are each uniquely beautiful. When you are virtuous, chaste, and morally clean, your inner beauty glows in your eyes and in your face. My grandfather used to say, "If you live close to God and His infinite grace—you won't have to tell, it will show in your face."[5]

As you read that quote, perhaps a woman you know who glows with the light of Christ came to mind. Whether or not you believe it, *you* might just be that same beautiful example for someone else. You never know who might be looking up to you, or who could use your smiles, your kindness, and your friendship. When you're living in overflow, you have enough of God's love for you stocked up in your own inner pantry so that you're freed up to give His love to others. You're living that inner Costco life. Bulk love for everyone!

Now, I know for some of us this is much easier said than done. We all deal with anxiety, self-doubt, self-criticism, insecurity, and perfectionism. I almost cancelled my first date with my soon-to-be husband, remember? If you're going through a moment of divine identity crisis right now, know that you are not alone. I'm right there with you. You don't have to act like you've got everything under control! Learning who you are and who you were meant to become is a life-long process, full of ups and downs. Letting our guard down and being honest about the battles we all face as women helps us forge real connections with others who may be going through similar things.

My counselor once asked me if I connect well with people who put on a front or try to look and act like they're perfect.

"Of course not!" I replied.

"What kind of people do you feel are easiest to connect with, Hailey?" she asked.

"People who are genuine. People who are down to earth. It's easier to connect with imperfect people who are trying than people who seem fake," I responded.

"Then what does that give you permission to be?" she asked, smiling.

Her words hit me like a ton of bricks. I whispered back, "Imperfect."

I then went home and wrote in my journal, "I give myself permission to be imperfect."

And I still do. Every single day! I feel the best about myself and can be the most generous toward others when I realize that we may be in different places on the path to spiritual confidence, but we're all walking it together. When I give myself grace, I'm empowered and feel steady in my own divine identity, and then I can extend that grace and space to others.

I do my best to try to draw close to God in every way I can, communicate with Him through prayer every single day, read the words of His scriptures, participate in my church meetings, love and take care of my family, and pray for and act on opportunities to serve His children, but I fall short and struggle with deep feelings of inadequacy. All. The. Time. In those hard moments, my confidence is restored when I remember that who I am is so much more than my failures or even the choices I make, and nothing will ever change the fact that I was destined to be a queen. God loves me infinitely, no matter what. Even though I may still be in the very early stages of His loving training, I know I'll get where He wants me to be if I get back up and keep trying!

A story recorded in the Old Testament tells of an amazingly courageous woman who stood firm in her divine identity, who also happens to be a queen. Her name was Esther. Esther was raised by her cousin Mordecai after her parents passed away. She had no mother of her own to look up to and learn from as she grew. When the king of Persia began searching for a new queen, Mordecai brought her to the palace, knowing that she was a gorgeous woman and she had a fair shot of attracting the King's attention (see Esther 2:7).

There must have been something about Esther that made her different, something that made her stand out from all of the other women around her, because "the king loved Esther above all the women, and she obtained grace and favour in his sight . . . so that he put the royal crown upon her head" (Esther 2:17).

Though she was a faithful Jew, Esther heeded the advice Mordecai had given her and did not reveal her faith to the king.

A power-hungry prince in the king's court named Haman became angry when Mordecai refused to bow before him. Haman complained to the king, claiming that there was a group of people refusing to obey the king's laws who deserved to be punished. He sought to destroy Mordecai and all his people— the Jews—unknowingly endangering the king's beloved wife, Queen Esther.

Mordecai asked Esther to plead with the king on behalf of her people. Esther was at first hesitant, explaining to Mordecai that by entering the inner court of the king uninvited, she would be breaking the law and would surely be put to death. But nowhere does it say in the scriptures that Esther at first doubted herself, thinking, "I'm just an orphan. I'm no queen. How can I possibly go before the king and risk my life? There's no way I can do this." If she did have thoughts such as these, they didn't last long.

Mordecai reminded Esther that the Lord might have had a greater purpose in her becoming queen, saying, "Who knoweth whether thou art come to the kingdom for such a time as this?" (Esther 4:14).

As queen, Esther could have stayed quietly hidden away in her luxurious palace and allowed her people to suffer to keep her secret safe. Instead she felt compassionate love for her brothers and sisters and knew that only she could convince the king to spare their lives. She knew what was required of her and couldn't just stand by and do nothing. She asked Mordecai to gather together all the nearby Jews to fast for her for three days, along with herself and her maidens. "And so will I go in unto the king, which is not according to the law: and if I perish, I perish," she said (Esther 4:16). She was so brave!

Where did this unwavering courage come from? Queen Esther's courage came from remembering who she was. She knew she was a queen, not because she was married to the king, but because she was a daughter of God. She knew if she fasted and prayed and asked her sisters and friends to do the same, the Lord would help her and would be by her side. She feared her God more than she feared man and exercised incredible faith to do what she knew was right.

Esther went before the king, prepared physically, spiritually, and emotionally, and anchored in her faith and courage. She felt calm and steady knowing that no matter what happened, her God was on her side. The king allowed her to enter his inner court and extended his merciful golden scepter, sparing her life and granting her whatever request she had come to make. Esther then hosted a feast for the king and for Haman, during which she revealed that she was a Jew. Haman's plot was foiled, and he was sent to the gallows, and Queen Esther was able to set an entire nation free.

I'll bet when Esther caught a glimpse of herself in the mirror before entering the king's court she didn't look at herself and say, "Oh my. Would you look at that blemish," or, "His last queen was so much prettier than I am." No way. When Esther met her own eyes in the mirror, she glowed with deep beauty and was able to face the king with steady confidence that she was a daughter of God, destined to be a queen.

What if we each paused every morning in the mirror before facing our day and said, "I am a daughter of God. He loves me, and I love Him"? I'm willing to try it. Will you?

As daughters of God, we can carry His light and love within each of our hearts. His love can then overflow like it did for Queen Esther into our own kingdoms—our workplaces, schools, church congregations, and especially into our homes.

One evening after praying to my Heavenly Father and expressing my gratitude for the incredible blessings He continually bestows upon me, I was overcome with a feeling of deep longing to be near Him again. I continued my prayer and said, "Father, I miss you. I miss being in your presence and learning from you. I miss feeling close to you."

As soon as I had offered those words in prayer, the most overwhelming, pure feeling of love spread through my whole being and filled my heart. His love and longing for me as His daughter was remarkable. It was just as powerful as if I had heard the words *I miss you too.*

I had never felt more connected to God as my father as I did in that moment of silent prayer. There have been other sacred moments throughout my life where I have been given glimpses of just how precious I am to my Heavenly Father. A feeling of serene peace and complete assurance fills me in those moments, creating memories and impressions that I rely on in moments when I start to forget who I am or question my worth.

If you have never prayed before, or never talked to God as your Heavenly Father, I encourage you to try it. Find a quiet place where you can be alone, kneel, and reverently pray to Him. He sees you. He knows you even better than you know yourself. Thank Him for the blessings that you have in your life, because all good things come from God. Ask Him what He thinks about you, whether He loves you. I know that as you do so, you will receive your own personal witness of your divine identity as a daughter of God. He will answer your sincere and heartfelt prayer in a way that is tailored to you. You are a daughter of a King, and though you may have forgotten, He will help you remember.

Feeling unified with our sisters starts with remembering who we are and gradually gaining confidence from our individual relationships with God.

NOTES

1. Brian K. Taylor, "Am I a Child of God?," *Ensign*, May 2018.
2. "Young Women Theme," *Young Women Personal Progress* (booklet, 2009), 3.
3. Boyd K. Packer, "To Young Women and Men," *Ensign*, May 1989, 54.
4. Elaine S. Dalton, "Remember Who You Are!," *Ensign,* May 2010.
5. Ibid.

Chapter 3

CELEBRATING DIFFERENCES

{ Hailey }

Remembering who we are is just the first step on the path to discovering what makes us unique and one of a kind. God lovingly created us to be different. There is only one YOU that exists in this universe! When we remember that we are daughters of God, we're then able to explore the kaleidoscope of traits, gifts, talents, interests, passions, and personality quirks He gave specifically to each of us. Those differences that set us apart and make us unique from every other woman in the world aren't meant to make us fall into the pit of comparison but instead are meant to be celebrated!

My favorite colors as a little girl were pink and purple, and I was adamant that none of my sisters shared my precious chosen colors. As a result, I have gone down in family lore as being the sole reason it took Allie and Mandi years to realize that their favorite colors were not, in fact, orange and yellow and black and white, as I'd assigned them to be. Even from a young age I wanted to be different and stand out from my sisters.

Being the oldest, I grew very impatient with them when it seemed they were trying to copy everything I did. "Imitation is the greatest form of flattery," Dad used to tell me, but that didn't stop me from trying to be the first and only one in our family to like horses, Jesse McCartney, and fettuccine alfredo. Maybe it's a trait of children who come from big families, but I liked having my own things.

Though I tried hard to stand out and be different in my preferences, style, and tastes, it just wasn't in the cards for me when it came to my physical appearance. Once we entered our teenage years, our heights evened out, and Allie, Mandi, and I started getting asked every time we met someone new if we were triplets. We share very similar physical traits, and people started having a very hard time telling us apart. Because of our similar build and hair color, Allie and I were often asked if we were twins, to which Mandi would respond, "What am I, the blonde cousin?"

Over the past couple of years, Lindsay has passed me in height, and now when we're together we are asked frequently if we are twins, despite our six-year age gap. Being the only daughter to inherit Mom's curly locks, I thought I had one saving identifiable trait that would set me apart, but many people still confuse me for Allie and Lindsay to this day. I can't tell you how often I hear things like, "Whoa . . . you all look exactly the same!" or "Lucy and Abby totally look like Mandi, while Lindsay looks just like Allie!"

My sisters are some of the most beautiful women I know, so it's a great compliment to be told that we look alike! But I think I speak for all of us when I say that despite our shared family traits, we couldn't be more different from each other in a lot of ways.

For many years, my sisters and I had a lot in common. We did literally everything together. We were inseparable. Our love for music, food, laughing, boys, and each other made it relatively easy to get along most of the time. I found a sense of security in knowing that if I liked something, my sisters would probably like it too.

As we grew older and started finding our own way, understanding and supporting my siblings when differences in opinion, choices, and perspectives started to crop up became challenging. I thought that obtaining unity in our family life and work required us to share similar views on everything and that I couldn't relate to my family members if we didn't share similar interests.

I have learned through my own experiences that the diversity that exists within our family is exactly what keeps life vibrant and interesting. It is possible to love each other in our differences. Each member of our family brings their own colorful threads that weave into our family dynamic and relationships.

Being the oldest, I feel that I have a unique stewardship, a deep desire to cherish and love each of my family members, to make sure they feel loved, seen, heard, and cared for. My approach has changed greatly as I've learned that differences, even if they seem huge, don't have to be a barrier to love. Holding space for our loved ones to be exactly who they are and trying to leave them better than we found them is what allows us to experience harmony in our relationships.

Though each of my sisters and I has at times been challenged in our relationships because of our differences, we've always been able to find common ground and come out of the hard moments even closer than we were before.

You have to let your sister know that she is enough no matter what. Who she is right now has to be enough for you to love her. Our job is to love our sisters exactly as they are without setting any expectations or conditions for her to meet to qualify for it.

This is unconditional love—something I'd always read scriptures about but never fully put into practice in my life until I understood this. To love my sisters unconditionally meant to love them as God loves them, to see them as He sees them. Though we were born sisters, our Heavenly Father created us to be individuals, each meant to fulfill our own mission and purpose. We were designed to be different.

To God, we always were and forever will be enough. We are always worthy of His unconditional, perfect love, so I knew He could help me love my sisters in the same way.

In comparing my sisters choices and life to my own, I had set my own expectations of who I thought they should be and how they should be moving through their lives. I can't use our differences as an excuse to put up a barrier and say, "Nope, I can't love them because we disagree on a lot of things, we do things differently, and we don't share the same viewpoints or passions. We are just too different from each other. Sorry!"

Our differences are what add zest and flavor to our families and relationships! We may never have everything in common as we walk through this life as sisters, but we can live differently from each other while still being respected and loved.

I want my sisters to know that for me, they will always be enough. That's what sisterhood is all about—living in unconditional love because we are all worthy of it right now, just as we are.

Being the oldest sister, I sometimes feel super out of touch with what's cool when I'm hanging out with my younger sisters. I mean, come on! It wasn't *that* long ago that I was in high school myself, but I can't keep up with the latest expressions, dance moves, and trends that my sisters are so on top of. Even though I sometimes feel like I'm ten years behind the times when I'm with them, we still find ways to relate and talk to each other and enjoy being together. They keep me feeling young! They have grown up to be really hilarious, fun-loving young women, and I'm so grateful I get to be a part of their lives as their older sister.

{ Mandi }

Growing up in a large family with so many sisters, we were constantly compared to each other. It didn't help that we sang together and, from a young age, regularly had the opinions of the online world thrown at us. (I think I was around thirteen when we posted our first video.) We basically grew up on YouTube, and our social media presence and videos stood in for the family photo albums and home videos that most people gather over time, except ours are available to the public. We continually had people comparing our looks, personality traits, talents, abilities, and even hobbies between us as sisters, most often straight to our faces or in rude comments we came across in our work.

Looking back, I realize we had every opportunity to listen to the opinions of others, and we could have chosen to let it create competition between us as siblings. Thankfully, my family and sisters seemed to be the only safe place in my life where the need to compare didn't exist. Our parents were always reminding us that we were each other's best friends and that each one of us had something unique to bring to the table that never detracted from the others. In our home, we not only learned to embrace each other's differences, but we try to celebrate them! And has it taken us years to figure that one out? Yes. Do we still have to make a constant, daily effort? Absolutely. But like my sister mentioned, we have learned over the years how to give each other (and ourselves) the breathing room to express our uniqueness and support each other's differences. And we're getting better and better as time goes on!

If my middle school and high school years weren't already awkward enough, my work life involving music with my sisters wasn't a huge help in building my personal confidence either. It seemed everywhere I went (whether it be school, friend's houses, the internet, or social media platforms), peers, adults, and strangers alike all had their own opinions of me and my sisters. They loved to tell us who they thought was the prettiest, funniest, smartest, or most talented. They had comments on our looks, voices, style, and even our religious views. We have seen and heard it all, and honestly, I can say now that I am so grateful for these experiences even at a young age, because it taught me a very valuable lesson: the only opinion that matters is from God.

In the confusion of trying to figure out who I was and how I felt about myself, I really came to understand what was meant in the scripture that says, "For the Lord seeth not as man seeth; for man looketh on the outward appearance, but the Lord looketh on the heart" (1 Samuel 16:7).

I have treasured and thought about an experience my mom shared with me during my teenage years when I was struggling with my own differences.

Growing up, my mom experienced a lot of bullying because of her physical appearance and found herself hardly able to make friends. She didn't feel very liked or even beautiful, and it was a lonely time for her.

A few years passed, and of course our sweet mom grew into a beautiful, confident young woman. She was on her high school and college cheer and dance teams and was loved by so many. The same kids who had made fun of her only a few years earlier wanted to be her friend, take her on dates, and compliment everything she did. Not only was my mom a great example of charity by never treating those who had treated her poorly with any disrespect, but she also was a great example of confidence by never letting her physical changes alter who she was inside. She has always gravitated toward people who come from different places and who don't speak the same language. She embraces people who don't look like everyone else and who may be quiet and shy.

My mom's story along with my own experience—I can totally relate to what some may call the "ugly duckling" stage, complete with braces, glasses, and yes, in my case, headgear—taught me the importance of finding others who seem lonely and forgotten and befriending them. I have learned so much from my mother about embracing the people around me who seem different and treating them with just as much, if not more, interest and respect as anyone else who may seem similar to me on the surface.

True beauty is not something you can see with your eyes, and it is truly incomparable to anything else. Our Heavenly Father made us all different; we look different, act different, like different things, and have different opinions. It is all by divine design, and we would be wise to embrace and accept what sets us apart from others. There is also much joy and enrichment that comes from allowing others to be themselves and learning from them.

Some of the greatest moments of my life have been with my family and sisters and have involved us being together in the studio, on the road, or even moments sitting and talking around the dinner table as a family. I cherish the music my sisters and

I have created together where Hailey comes up with a beautiful guitar part, Allie kills it on her vocals, and I arrange the background harmony.

If we were too busy comparing our abilities and different strengths to each other, I know it would have been a lot less enjoyable, maybe even discouraging, if we had allowed ourselves to think we weren't enough simply because we didn't have the same strength as another sibling. I will always be grateful for those *magic moments* that occur when we come together to strengthen each other where we are weak, both in and out of the studio.

We would do well to remember those things in our daily interactions with our family members, friends, and even strangers around us. If we were all the same, my goodness, this world would be so boring! I have learned that the more accepting I am of the differences in myself and others, the more opportunities I have in learning and growing personally.

The question we must ask ourselves is this: How do we not only embrace difference but also celebrate it? I think the answer is simple. As sisters in Zion, we must always encourage each other. We must seek to build one another up in both word and deed.

Think about someone in your life who makes you feel like you're on cloud nine every time you're around them. Notice how your interactions are almost always happy and mood boosting. I'm sure this is the same person you think to call first when you receive some good news you want to share, and I'd even bet this person is always there when you need a helping hand.

For me, the people who do this for me in my life always, without fail, bring out the best in me and give me the freedom to feel like I can completely be myself. I admire these individuals and make a conscious effort to try to reciprocate the goodness I receive from them in my interactions with others. It always feels good to be around people who celebrate *your* differences, literally cheering you on in your life endeavors. I always feel refreshed and inspired after being around individuals this way, because it is a great reminder of how much more enriching my interactions with my family could be if I allowed my siblings to feel this same kind of celebration from me.

I will openly admit that I don't always feel like a box of chocolates and a dozen roses when my sisters progress without me. I'd like to say it's just me not wanting to miss out on something, and not necessarily my pride, but I think we all know that's not always the case. We did everything together, from writing music to eating meals at the same table, for so long that when the time came for our lives to start taking a different course, I had a very difficult time embracing the changes.

When my two older sisters, my closest friends, got married and moved away from me, I really struggled with my identity and purpose. Like, come on, we're supposed to be single together forever and be little studio rats cranking out music until we're so old we can't even remember each other's names!

I took things personally when decisions came between me or a spouse and when my sisters had a shift in priorities that no longer involved our combined goals. Honestly, it created a divide between me and my sisters that I never thought possible, and I absolutely hated it! After struggling with my own insecurities around the situation, I finally realized something that bridged the gap for me and my sisters. One person's success will never, ever, EVER take away from yours.

A quote often used in our household by Jeffrey R. Holland states, "Obviously we suffer a little when some *misfortune* befalls *us,* but envy requires us to suffer all *good fortune* that befalls *everyone* we know! What a bright prospect that is—downing another quart of pickle juice every time anyone around you has a happy moment! To say nothing of the chagrin in the end, when we find that God really is both just and merciful, giving to all who stand with Him 'all that he hath,' as the scripture says. So lesson number one from the Lord's vineyard: coveting, pouting, or tearing down does *not* elevate *your* standing, nor does demeaning someone else improve your self-image. So be kind, and be grateful that God is kind. It is a happy way to live."[1]

I am totally learning as I go here, but it is safe to say I now have a better understanding that growth and change for anyone and everyone is such a great thing! It is amazing to watch the people you love and respect the most try new things and excel in all areas of their life. Life can be so enjoyable and happy when you choose not to drink the pickle juice but instead celebrate the accomplishments and achievements of others, especially within your family relationships.

I have learned that it's silly to not grow with and move forward alongside your friends and family. Be happy for them. It's not fun for anyone if you choose to distance yourself just because you experience feelings of inadequacy or insecurity. Just learn from my mistakes and take my word for it, that encouraging the people you love to spread their wings and fly will also make you feel like you're the one flying!

Life will take a different course for you, each of your friends, and every single one of your siblings. And if you have the eyes to see it, I know you will find your differences will be the very things that help you grow closer to others around you and will inspire you to reach your own personal potential. Truly we are more similar to each other than not, and as for my family, celebrating our differences has become the very thing that has strengthened our sister bond and unified us together as a family. So embrace it in others, and celebrate them daily!

NOTE

1. Jeffrey R. Holland, "The Laborers in the Vineyard," *Ensign*, May 2012.

Chapter 4

LIKE MOTHER, LIKE DAUGHTER

{ Mandi }

Near-death experiences have a way of changing the way you look at things. I had heard before that death was peaceful, but there I sat in the kitchen of our home in North Carolina, unable to move or concentrate on anything but my breathing, thinking, "Why do I feel like I'm dying?"

Just two days before, I had competed in my last race on my high school track team, and though I was present to race, I felt I had let my coach and team down for having to drop out of my first event after the very first lap. I remember my dad saying it probably wasn't normal that I couldn't make it one lap, and I probably should have been more concerned that before that, the more I ran, the tighter my lungs became, but I never thought to assume the worst.

Feeling lightheaded and in a daze, my mom entered the kitchen.

"Are you okay?" she asked when she saw me. "You don't look very good."

She immediately dropped what she was doing and came to my side. I explained to her I was having another one of those weird breathing episodes, which were becoming more and more frequent, but this time jogging down the driveway was all it took to make me feel like my lungs were about to explode! We decided it was time to go to the doctor.

I spent that night in urgent care with my mom while they ran test after test on me—checking my heart rate, blood levels, lung volume, breathing capacity—you name it, they did it! After monitoring me into the early morning, the doctor thought it best for me to return home and come back later for one more test. Depending on the results, my options were to get a CAT scan at the hospital or start using an inhaler for what they thought might be exercise-induced asthma.

My mom, who had been up since 5:30 that morning, and who had spent an entire day driving eight people around to their various activities, calmly took me home. The next day she was up with breakfast and a smile, and after a quick pep talk with her and my dad, we were back at the urgent care.

My resting heart rate had skyrocketed. Still calm and encouraging, my mom drove into the city to the closest hospital. No one knows better than my mother just how much I hate the doctor. She is well aware that I pass out even at the thought of a needle and that I'm the kind of kid who will wait until my wisdom teeth are all the way in before I even mention to her that my jaw kind of hurts. I will literally do anything to avoid being poked. When the nurse walked in with an IV and a needle the size of lead in a mechanical pencil, my mom smiled and grabbed my hand. Distracting me with questions, funny stories, and new recipe ideas, she spent the afternoon with me as doctors ran more tests and we waited for results. I remember the radiologists called in from the back, and a nurse handed my mom the phone.

Her eyes got wide, and all she said was, "Really?" and then she started to cry. She quickly composed herself and told me they had found several substantial blood clots in my lungs. I was immediately wheeled to the emergency room, my mind spinning.

It was a long week to follow. More testing, hospital transfers in an ambulance, teams of nurses in and out of my room, shots, shots, and more shots. And there my mom was, every day by my side and every night sleeping in the chair by the window. She drove an hour each way to get comfortable PJs, books, and blankets for me from home. She raided the hospital cafeteria for the chocolate chip cookies anytime I craved them and swatted at the nurses anytime they tried to draw blood places other than through my IV. We couldn't stop laughing when we tried to get the machinery unhooked from me faster than the laxatives were running through my bed-ridden body and when my heart-monitor would begin beeping incessantly every time we tried to fall asleep. (We were both ready to throw that thing out the window!)

A few days later, I was able to return home.

I will never forget the first time I had to give myself my blood-thinner injection. Literally my worst nightmare. I was on my bed, my mom kneeling on the ground resting her hand on my leg. We counted to three, she hugged me when I was finished, and we celebrated with some chocolate when I didn't pass out.

For two weeks straight, she drove me an hour to the doctor's to get my blood levels checked, and then once a week for seven months to follow. Not once did she ever complain or act like I was an inconvenience or a burden.

The weekend I came home from the hospital was a time of deep reflection for me. My doctors had told me multiple times most people with clots don't usually make it, and they had never seen a case like mine where someone so young had them. For a young teenager, it was hard to grasp that my life had almost stopped there. I knew if it had, I wouldn't have lived up to my potential.

The greatest lesson I learned was how blind I had been to the love and devotion of my mother. Before my blood clot experience, I was beginning to feel distant from my mom—like I knew best and I didn't need the help and advice she had to give. I often responded to my mother's comments and questions with an annoyed attitude, and I lacked the respect she deserved from me. I overlooked her generosity, care, and sacrifice she so freely gave to me and my siblings. From the hospital bed and through the first week of recovery at home, I thought about everything that had just happened. I couldn't ignore the feelings of gratitude I felt when I would wake up in the hospital room in the early hours of the morning to see my mom situated uncomfortably in a chair trying to sleep. I felt guilty every time I thought of moments where I didn't treat my mom with the same respect and love she constantly showed me.

That weekend home from the hospital, I felt overwhelmed with the love I had for my mom, the gratitude I felt for everything she did for me, and her devotion and care for me. I felt it so much, I remember going into her room and just hugging her and crying, telling her how much I was grateful for her. What a shame that it took this experience for me to acknowledge the way I should have always been treating my mother!

It was a turning point in our relationship and a paradigm shift for me to realize my parents were just as much there for me as my friends and siblings. I wish it hadn't taken me so long to recognize the value of my parents' involvement in my life and the wisdom and experience they had to offer. From that point forward, I began to see my mom as someone who would give anything for me, and I wanted to treat her with more love and respect. I'm grateful I had this experience to help me see my mother clearly, as the amazing woman that she is. This outlook has carried me and helped me connect with my mom and know that I can turn to her for help and advice.

I'm grateful I learned this as a teenager because it has helped me in many ways since. Seeing my mother for the experienced and wise mentor that she is has been a great blessing to me, and I often learn from her past experiences and stories. Being close to women who share their experiences and the lessons they have learned can become a great strength to you. Their stories and advice will help you navigate life and will make you stronger in the process.

Just a few years ago I began dating a great guy, and I was really excited about the idea of having a future with him. I found myself falling fast yet being in a bit of a pickle. We didn't share all the same values and priorities, and I knew that to be with him I would have to compromise a few things that were important to me. I didn't know what to do: our relationship was progressing quickly, and I knew things would only get harder if I chose to move forward with him.

For the first time in my life, I went to my mom for relationship advice. She sat with me and listened as I weighed the pros and cons out loud, and we had a great conversation. She told me about a situation she had growing up that was similar to mine that I had never heard her talk about before, and it gave me the courage to end the relationship. I was so grateful for her guidance and for her sharing her experience. It helped me make the right decision at the right time, and I have been able to stay friends with this guy—which was also important for me at the time. I wondered why I hadn't gone to my mom sooner for dating advice and why I hadn't involved her more in my concerns about past boyfriends. She had so much life experience and so many stories

I hadn't even heard, because I never asked! It was a great learning experience for me and a great bonding moment I had with my mother as I opened up to her.

To get to know more experienced influences in your life, spend quality time with these women. Like with my mother, asking questions, having open conversation, and connecting with her on a deeper level gave me fresh perspective for managing my own life. When applying these principles to our interactions with other women, we can gain insight and assistance from those who have greater life experience. There is so much that can be learned from another's life. We just need to take the time to hear it.

For me and my mom, most of our interactions together revolve around food. We are both incredibly passionate about both the food we eat and the food we make. My relationship with my mom isn't all serious. Though I know I can come to her if I need advice or help, I also know I can go to her when I need a friend or a good laugh.

One of my favorite memories with my mom was after one of our family Sunday-night dinners. Everyone had gone home, my younger siblings were going to bed, and it was just me and my mom left in the kitchen talking together. Mid-conversation my mom randomly interjected, "I need some chocolate," and I responded, "Yup. Me too," and then the next thing I knew we were in the kitchen whipping together a gourmet Texas sheet cake at like twelve o'clock (and when I say "we," I really mean more like I watched my mom make it, and I licked the spoons). It was such a fun night and was one of my favorite moments with her. It was such a simple thing, but I was so grateful for that moment of quality time I had with her, and that she made time for me late at night in her busy schedule, when she still had all my younger siblings to be around and take care of.

With this experience, my mother taught me another valuable lesson. Sometimes we have to let things go to focus on things of eternal importance. Family is one of those prime examples. To develop lasting bonds and relationships with our parents and siblings, we first have to be willing to invest in the time it will take to do so. Staying up a few extra minutes to bake a cake or sitting down to talk instead of checking off another task on a "to-do" list makes all the difference in the world in building strong family relationships. Those little moments become the very framework of a strong family foundation later in life as we build trust, patience, understanding, and memories together.

Life gets busy. As we get older, we find we have more demands placed on us that often distract from things that are truly important. In my family, we have this running joke that *mom is always down*. She is so fun and spontaneous, and all of us know if you were to randomly call her up and say you wanted to go do something fun, she would be there. One of the best trips I had with my mom happened about a year ago. I was in the middle of moving apartments, and I had to be out of my room that weekend. I had been trying to pack all week, and I had just one day to finish. I remember getting a phone call from my mom around 9:30 at night in the middle of my packing that went like this:

"Hi, Manda!"

"Hey, Mom. What are you guys up to?"

"Ummm, well, Lucy and I want to go to California, and we're going to leave tomorrow morning. I think we're going to go to Disneyland. You want to come?"

And that was that. My angel roommate let me shove my remaining things in her room, and the next morning at seven, we were on the road to Disneyland! It was such a fun trip with just me, my mom, and Lucy, and it was one for the books! I loved how spontaneous it was, so like my mother.

Though my mom and I can be similar, we too have our opposites. Where she can be carefree and spontaneous, I tend to gravitate toward set schedules and color-coordinated planners. I've found moments like spontaneous Disney trips and impromptu moves can initially stress me out. The irony lies in the aftereffect. I have never regretted changing my plans to make more time for the people I love. It's those moments and events that I treasure for years to come and that make me feel a deeper connection with the people I experience them with. When I think about mother-daughter relationships, I feel very blessed to have a wonderful mother who is a great example in my life. Her example has always been a huge testimony builder and strength to me. There is no gap between what she says she knows and what she does.

My entire life I knew that my mom's advice could be trusted because she lived it. If she said she knew dressing a certain way would help show the respect we had for ourselves and others, I knew she knew it because she was dressed that way. I knew she meant it when she said she loved attending church meetings, loved serving others, and loved the Lord because she went every Sunday, gave her all to church callings, and was always doing good for other people. I felt it was important to strive to be obedient because I knew my mother found it important. I was drawn to the temple because my mom always talked about her love for being there and how much she knew it blessed her life and the entire family. I drew from her strength, and her example helped shape who I am today. There are many women around us who do the same.

I have felt blessed to also have the influence of other mother-like figures who have strengthened my faith and been individuals I hope to become like. Two of these women were my church leaders growing up in North Carolina.

Windy Sabin was my Sunday School teacher through my middle school years, my Young Women teacher at the beginning of high school, and my seminary teacher my senior year. What a woman she is! If I could describe her accurately to you, the best word I can think of is energetic. She has a zest for life, and her excitement and passion for the simple things is completely contagious. She is beautiful and vibrant, loves the Lord, and has so much gospel knowledge; I adored every second I had around her.

I felt strengthened as a youth hearing about her battle cancer in her twenties and the lessons she had learned about family and how much she loved hers. Her refreshing personality was exciting to be around. She took me under her wing during difficult times and was my best friend at church—she never made me feel like our ages made any difference, and I absolutely love her for that. She taught me how to drive stick-shift in her bright yellow jeep and let me stay at her house for a week before meeting up with my family for our summer vacation in another state. We stayed up until 2:00 a.m. making tomato soup and grilled cheese, and her childhood stories would make me just laugh. When I attended a difficult year at girl's camp and experienced bullying from some of the other girls and leaders, I walked to the other side of the campground and cried to her in her tent. She totally stuck up for me when I didn't have the courage to do it myself, and she took quite a bit of heat for it.

We laugh about it now, but I was so grateful for her love and genuine concern for me, as if I were one of her own kids. She may never know the magnitude of her example and its effect in my life, but I drew so much strength from her love of the gospel, and I fed off her confidence when mine was low. I will be grateful for her influence in my life as long as I live! She's someone I want my kids to meet and know, and I will forever be grateful for the love and kindness she extended and continues to give to me in my life as we have remained close.

Another church leader who is a motherly figure to me is an incredible woman named Sharmyn Mitchell. Sister Mitchell is wonderful; to me she is the definition of beautiful. She married in her early forties, and though she has no children of her own, she is a mother to many. Sister Mitchell has a deep love for the Savior and a unique view of God's children and of the world because of her many travel experiences. She has incredible life stories of her adventures living abroad, of her faith as she navigated life, and of the Lord's plan for her. She is always smiling. She has a soft, caring heart and a gentle soul, and she is the perfect balance of smart and funny. Everything she touches becomes beautiful, from her house and her garden to the people she serves. I have wanted to be like her ever since I met her in church as a young girl. She has the gift of making everyone feel recognized and remembered, and she always seems to be at the major crossroads of my life. Whether by reaching out to see how I'm doing in a text or flying out to arrange flowers and make food for a sister's wedding, Sister Mitchell is always there for me and for my mom and sisters. She is one of the greatest examples I know of charity and selflessness, and I hope to be as motherly and faithful as she is one day.

Mother-daughter relationships, in all forms, are a beautiful gift to us in this life. They are meant to be a source of stability and dependability for each of us. As M. Russell Ballard so beautifully stated, "My dear young women, with all my heart I urge you not to look to contemporary culture for your role models and mentors. Please look to your faithful mothers for a pattern to follow. Model yourselves after *them*, not after celebrities whose standards are not the Lord's standards and whose values may not reflect an eternal perspective. Look to your mother. Learn from her strengths, her courage, and her faithfulness. Listen to her. She may not be a whiz at texting; she may not even have a Facebook page. But when it comes to matters of the heart and the things of the Lord, she has a wealth of knowledge. As you approach the time for marriage and young motherhood, she will be your greatest source of wisdom. No other person on earth loves you in the same way or is willing to sacrifice as much to encourage you and help you find happiness—in this life and forever."[1] I know his words are true!

It's interesting as you grow older how your perspective of your mother, and other motherly influences, will change. You will, if you haven't already, get to a point where you realize how human both of your parents are. How human we all are. They too have goals and dreams, and believe it or not, they're not perfect! They try their best, and of course they want the best for you. Like any relationship, having patience and understanding for one another will keep your relationship growing. I often look at my mom for the amazing service she renders to all. I like talking to her about *her* dreams and goals and hearing all the ideas that go through her head. I feel connected with her, and I feel that I can relate to her when I take the time to get to know her and her stories.

I've learned over the years just how similar we are. I used to deny it, but now that I know more about her, I realize my mother is who I want to emulate.

In addition to asking my parents about themselves, I have also been trying to be better at expressing my gratitude and love more openly with them. They are great at doing so with me, always complimenting me, saying they love me, and asking about what I hope for in my future. I'm realizing it helps my connection with them to do the same. My new favorite thing is leaving notes expressing my love and appreciation the moment I think of it. I've found that not withholding those words of affirmation will help you grow closer to your family members and parents. It has helped me be more aware of the sacrifices my parents make for me every single day, for they are many.

Keep close to your mothers or the mother-figures in your life who fill that role for you and inspire you. And remember as you grow older and you become those women for others and mothers of your own family to never underestimate your influence—especially your influence as a woman. Throughout your life, your influence will extend to others as you carry the role of a daughter, friend, sister, mother, and even mentor. You will continue the circle of exemplary womanhood and bless the lives of many, just as your mother and the nurturing women in your life have blessed you. Embrace your relationship with your mom with understanding and a loving heart, and begin now to strive to be more like the strong women you admire most in your life. We don't have to be the same ages, in the same stages of life, or even blood relatives to be sister strong together. Finding and maintaining mother and mother-figure relationships will create a support structure that will uplift and sustain you in all stages of your life.

NOTE

1. M. Russell Ballard, "Mothers and Daughters," *Ensign*, May 2010.

Chapter 5

FINDING YOUR TRIBE

{ Hailey }

We all want to feel like we belong. We all want to find our people. I believe the tribe of sisters that we choose to belong to can have a great impact on who we become, for better or for worse.

It might be helpful to ask yourself a few questions about the women you're closest to in your life. Who are the five women you spend the most time with? Are they members of your family? Are they friends? What character traits do they possess that have influenced your perspectives or behavior? Do you feel safe, loved, and free to be yourself in their presence? How have they helped shape you into the person that you are? Despite their imperfections or weaknesses, do they lift and encourage you to be your best self? How do they treat and talk about others?

If any of the answers to these questions make you feel a little uncomfortable, it might be time to reevaluate your tribe and which women you are allowing to be in your most direct circle of influence.

For some of us, the most influential women in our lives are going to be the people we live with, our relatives or other people at home. Remember, we don't have control over the choices our sisters make, but God asks us to love them anyway. For some of us, our relationships with our sisters, mother, or the other women we live with may look like a Wednesday night cake-decorating class at Michaels (cue the elevator music playing softly in the background and cordial chitchat). But for the rest of us, our home life might feel like World War III is constantly playing itself out in our living room.

Your current home situation might be a place of discord, chaos, and heartbreak. Even if this is the case, know that you don't have to let your home life become your *whole* life. You can seek out and surround yourself with other women outside of your home who can serve as sisters to you in your time of need. They might be imperfect, but if they lift, encourage, and love you and are trying their best to live a good life, they are meant to be in your tribe.

Though not all of us come from ideal family situations, we know that God designed our families specifically for each of us to grow in an environment that would test and refine us. I was sent to my family as the oldest sibling for a reason, just as Lucy was sent to be the youngest. All ten of us were meant to be related, to share experiences together, and to walk side by side through the ups and downs of life. We have specific roles only we can fill, and we need each other.

One of the most indirectly influential women in my life is Marjorie Pay Hinckley, the wife of President Gordon B. Hinckley. Though we never had the chance to meet, I feel like I know her. When I read her speeches and books, I laugh and cry as if she's telling me her stories herself. Her wit and feisty personality combined with her optimism and unshakable testimony made her a force to be reckoned with. Her insights into family life always leave me feeling encouraged and hopeful.

"Being a son or daughter," she once said, "is probably the hardest role you have to play. Home is where you are loved the most and act the worst. But I have come to the conclusion that it is in the home where we are tested the most. Most of us have developed a pretty good set of company manners that we exercise at school and socials and church and other places, but it is what we are at home that tells the true story of what we really are. The family unit is fundamental. I wonder if this was so there would be some area where we would function with our guard down so that the Lord could see what we really are."[1]

If it's true that the home is the place where the Lord sees what we really are, then heaven help us all! We all slam doors, call each other names, test out our favorite curse words on each other, kick each other under the dinner table, and break household items both on accident and in attempt to injure someone else.

While focusing on our frustrating and difficult family moments can be discouraging, it's important to remember that the Lord also sees the small, passing moments that no one else sees, the sweet experiences that bind our hearts together.

He sees when we help our little sister with her homework before doing our own. He sees us wake up countless times in the middle of the night to comfort our crying children. He sees our hugs, our kisses, our *I love you*s, and the tears we cry together. He counts the cups of water we fill up at bedtime, our cheers from the sidelines, and the pages of the picture books we turn. He sees us laughing together and laughs with us. When we are living in disharmony, are experiencing betrayal or loss, or are without any family to call our own, His heart aches with ours. He hears our prayers of heartbreak and sorrow and cries with us. God is in our families because we are His family.

From the time we were very little, my parents held family home evening. They would teach us a gospel lesson, we would sing songs and play games together, and Mom usually baked something sweet for us to enjoy afterward. One of the most impressionable parts of those younger years was the song we would sing together at the close of our family nights every single week. We would all kneel down in a circle on our living room floor, and before offering a prayer and going to bed, we would join hands and sing together.

> I have a family here on earth.
> They are so good to me.
> I want to share my life with them through all eternity.
> Families can be together forever
> Through Heavenly Father's plan.
> I always want to be with my own family,
> And the Lord has shown me how I can.[2]

I can still remember holding my little siblings' tiny hands in mine and singing those words as I looked around at the people who mattered most to me. My family was, and still is, my whole world, my tribe. Those same feelings of peace, love, and unity that filled my heart as a child return every time I hear or sing this song in church. I can never get through it without feeling overwhelmed with love for my family.

For me, I've been blessed to call the six women in my immediate family my tribe. My mom and sisters are my best friends, my support group, my book and supper clubs. They are my people. But I also have made the effort to seek out other incredible women that I can trust, ask for advice, or go to dinner with every so often. Even if your immediate family or next-door neighbors aren't people you can count on, turn to, and grab ice cream with, there are so many good and faithful women out there who are just like you! You might have to be the one to seek them out, but once you find them, you will cherish their friendship and sisterhood.

I'll admit, it's taken me many years to find the few women outside of my family who I now consider my tribe, women I really connect with. I was always pretty shy when it came to making new friends, and in a lot of cases, I didn't feel like I needed friendships because I already had my sisters as my built-in best friends. I would wait until I was invited, and up until a couple of years ago, rarely did I extend invitations myself.

Right after my husband and I got married, we moved into an apartment complex where we didn't know anyone. One of our neighbors was another young, recently married couple. One night, Brooklyn and her husband invited us over for dinner. Little did I know that her invitation would lead to the discovery that she is definitely one of my long-lost soul sisters! I'm so grateful that she not only invited us over and fed us a delicious meal but also put herself out there and invited me into her life. We discovered that we had so much in common, including the fact that we were the oldest sisters in our family.

Brooklyn's simple invitation has turned into a beautiful friendship between us that is a great blessing in my life and will continue to be for years to come. I try to follow her example by extending the invitation myself to women who might need a friend, women who might in fact be members of my tribe. And it starts with a simple smile and a few questions, and maybe an invitation for dinner.

Finding your tribe might require stepping outside your comfort zone to find a group of people, or even just one person, who you connect well with. If you love baking, track down the girl who brought the amazing salted caramel chocolate brownies to the church Christmas party and ask her to teach you how to make them. If you're a novel writer, join a writer's group at your local library. Not only will you get amazing feedback on your work, but you'll form friendships with ladies who share similar interests. If you are a big movie fan, host a girls' night at your house and invite a couple girls in your apartment complex or neighborhood over to bake cookies you can eat while watching a chick flick.

Even if it's uncomfortable at first, make a habit of turning to the girl sitting next to you in class or at church and ask her a few questions. Sit next to the wise woman who offers really insightful comments in your Sunday School class and get to know her. You never know where your small talk could lead. You might even discover that you share something really valuable in common that could lead to an amazing, trusting, lifelong friendship. She could totally be an influential mentor, a member of your tribe, and you may not even know it yet!

If, like me, you have been blessed to be a part of a tribe of wonderful women within your family, it's important to remember that it's okay if you experience internal disputes, mutiny, or power struggles. And it is totally normal to feel like the relationships you value the most are also some of the greatest challenges you face in your life!

I am a sister, a daughter, a wife, a friend, and someday a mother, connected with eternal bonds to people who knew me before I was born and will continue to be mine after I die. From my relationships with my sisters and friends, I'm continually learning in ways that are most effective for me how to love people just as they are.

You were sent to your tribe, your family, because it's where you would be tested the most, but also where you could be loved the most and where you could make the greatest difference in this world. I know this just as surely now as I did when I was a young girl surrounded by the people I love the most, singing that song each week on family night. You're already a part of an incredible tribe of women in this world because of your divine lineage as a daughter of God. He will send more of his faithful daughters into your life, giving you sisters by birth or by friendship, so that you can become sister strong together.

NOTES

1. Marjorie Pay Hinckley and Virginia H. Pearce, *Glimpses into the Life and Heart of Marjorie Pay Hinckley* (Salt Lake City: Deseret Book, 1999), 60.
2. "Families Can Be Together Forever," *Children's Songbook*, 188.

Chapter 6

LAUGHING IT OFF

{ Hailey }

There are a few surefire ways to get the Gardiner family to laugh. Give us an inopportune funny moment when we're *not* supposed to laugh and we're guaranteed to all be silently holding back giggles. Anything uncomfortable or awkward—falls, performances gone wrong, movies, social interactions, misspellings, and mispronunciations—we're all about it. And we love retelling those stories to each other just so we can laugh together. We have the same sense of humor and can totally appreciate the opportunities to laugh at life's awkward and unfortunate moments as sisters and as a family.

Several years back, we were playing our first headlining show in Los Angeles at a little club called Genghis Cohen. It was a sold-out show, and we were blown away that there was a room full of people who liked us enough to actually *pay* for tickets to come see us play live. While we warmed up and got ready in a room off to the side of the stage, we could hear the crowd talking and laughing through an open doorway. I remember the nerves started to kick in, and a few minutes before we were supposed to go on, we decided we needed to find a restroom.

The only way for us to get out of the venue without walking right down the middle of the crowd was to go through a side stage door that exited onto the street, allowing the audience to see us for a split second as we moved between the rooms.

There's so much anticipation in waiting for an artist to make their entrance onstage—I mean, can't we all just admit we totally cried when Taylor Swift emerged in her glittery gown the first time we saw her in concert? Despite the risks of ruining that moment, we decided to chance it.

Our Dad held the door for us, acting as our impromptu bodyguard. Allie, Mandi, and I ducked out of the room and moved as fast as we could through the exit. The small audience started screaming, and I got a little too hasty, whipping around to wave back at them. In that split second, I took my eye off the prize and totally tripped over the doorway.

It was like a movie: flailing limbs, a flying pouf of curly hair, and I was down on my knees out on the street outside. I biffed it HARD. My dad and sisters grabbed my arms and tried to help me up, but I couldn't even stand because we were all laughing!

What are the chances I'd totally bail in front of a group of people who were seeing us in person for the first time? I could have been mortified, super self-conscious about my first impression, but it was just too funny not to laugh at! I had scraped a hole in my leggings but wore them onstage anyway, and later in the show we made some pretty great jokes about breaking a leg and my glorious faceplant. My potentially embarrassing moment actually lightened up the show and a situation where we could have been really nervous, helping us feel connected to a crowd of strangers. They were there to cheer me on and support me, whether I made a perfectly dramatic Taylor Swift glittery entrance or not.

{ Mandi }

OH, MY GOODNESS! It brings me to tears just thinking about Hailey falling! I don't know why she has the worst luck with that, but I'll tell you what, the best part about our sister humor is if one person is on the ground, we all go down together and just lie there laughing so hard we can't get up.

{ Hailey }

Speaking of tears, when I was about four years old and Allie was about two, we busted out my pre-school plastic box of school supplies and started playing "haircut" with my little purple scissors. Allie sat in the rocking chair in our living room and I snipped off a couple inches of her already-short hair. She looked in an imaginary mirror, told me "I love it!" pretended to thank me graciously, and then would "go home" before returning to the hairdresser. This happened several times, and I obliged her with my well-trained hand, snipping until her hair was pretty much at her scalp. We then had some fun tossing the clumps of hair at each other before deciding it was my turn to get a new 'do.

The scissors were poised at the top of my ponytail and we were about to chop the whole thing off when Mom came into the room and ruined our plans.

"What have you DONE?!" she shrieked.

I don't remember much after that, aside from being swept up and promptly taken to my room, and then someone at the door later in the day who rudely asked me if I'd like to be a hairdresser when I grew up when she saw Allie's bald head.

I was not impressed.

Poor Allie had to wear those obnoxious bow-and-faux-flower-laden hats of the '90s until her hair grew back. And Mom cried over the ordeal, but I've become a hairstyling legend and the source of much laughter as we retell and remember this story. Sometimes we gotta wait for the hair to grow back before it becomes funny, right? If it's hard to find it funny now, give it time, and you'll probably be able to laugh at it down the road.

{ Mandi }

One thing we admire about our mom is her ability to laugh instead of getting upset. It has been our saving grace ever since we were kids. We all knew that if you could just get mom to laugh and see the humor in our shenanigans, you might avoid getting in trouble altogether.

I'll never forget my mom having to turn around for a few seconds to hide her laughter while trying to get our little brother Tim to confess he had gone without permission to the gas station and stained the carpet walkway with his blue Slurpee. Or the many times all eight of us kids have broken out into improvised jingles when we want her to stop for ice cream on family road trips. If I had a dollar for every time I've heard my parents say, "Stop singing off key or you're not going to be able to harmonize in real life," I'd be so rich!

Our mom and dad try really hard to keep straight faces, but all us kids know if we can just get our mom to crack a smile—it's over. That road trip is going to end with laughter *and* ice cream. Unless one of Tim's ear-shattering falsetto notes *actually* does upset someone.

{ Hailey }

Our other little brother, Ben, was known as "the destroyer" when he was a toddler. He would lock himself in our bedrooms and just wreak havoc on whatever he could get his hands on. One day I found him in my bedroom, scissors in hand. Luckily the only person he'd injured was Captain Jack Sparrow. Ben had cut his head right off of the poster I'd left on my bedroom floor. His scissors had also found their way up my curtains and across his little bangs, leaving him with a peacock fringe until it grew back. I'm noticing a trend; maybe the real moral of story here is to hide the scissors.

Allie and Mandi had a huge dollhouse in their bedroom made up of all these tiny, intricate pieces and miniature furniture that had taken them hours to build. Within a few minutes, Ben could decimate the place, somehow even having time and patience to rip each individual flower off its plastic stem. We could have been so mad at him, but I remember all of us just laughing at the skill with which he took things apart and at my headless Jack Sparrow. Ben is now an incredible artist and master Lego builder, so all of that breaking must have helped him gain some of the awesome skills he has now.

{ Mandi }

It's not so easy to laugh when you're the one who has to put all THREE stories of the dollhouse back together with no instruction book! Just the fact that he was so thorough still cracks me up!

{ Hailey }

Sometimes the only way to keep everybody cool with each other is to just find something to laugh about. I keep a running list of funny things our siblings and parents say in my phone. Reading through it never fails to make me laugh and brings back the moments I would have forgotten about if I hadn't jotted them down. It's an awesome practice I'd highly encourage you to start if you don't write funny things down already!

{ Mandi }

My sisters and I have what we call "no shame." As in we don't take ourselves too seriously and we act like FOOLS when we're together, often forgetting that there are other people around when we're in public. Our poor mother.

I guess it might be a good thing that we're able to be ourselves whether we're at home, out in public, or filming videos—what you see is definitely what you get. However, sometimes our funny sister moments happen in the worst possible places, at the worst possible times, and usually when we're supposed to be the most professional or reverent. If anyone is most likely to get the bad case of the giggles at the most inconvenient of times, it will almost always be me.

{ Hailey }

I can attest to that! Mandi has a signature way of letting us know when she's holding back laughter. She'll no-so-subtly dig her elbow into whoever is closest to her, and we'll see her lips pursed into in a tight, forced smile and know she's dying inside.

{ Mandi }

No matter how many hours we practice, how many times we sing through a song, or how many shows we perform with the same set, my mind spaces *at least* once during every performance. My sisters have this running joke that if anyone is going to forget lyrics, it will be me.

One performance I remember very distinctly (I hate to admit how often this happens) happened during our set at this really intimate restaurant in Hawaii. We were singing a cover we have sung together literally hundreds of times, which also happens to be one of my favorites to sing with my sisters live. I had my eyes closed, and I was swaying and everything—just really lost in the moment. We sang through the intro, the first verse, and the first chorus, and then hit this down spot before the next verse with some pretty three-part harmony. Then I skipped straight to the *bridge*! A couple lines in, I came back to reality and realized the song was about to end!

My eyes shot open, and I turned my head quickly to give my sisters a, "Oh no! How do we fix this even though I can't say anything to you because we're in the middle of a song?" look, and that's when we totally lost it. Bless my sisters, they just had to go with it!

They tried to keep up their harmony for one final chorus, but we couldn't even look at each other without laughing! Our thirty-second song ended in giggly, choppy words and heads in the hands, and when the audience gave us a slow clap, we busted up even more! None of us could look at each other the rest of the set, because if we saw one crack of a smile on the other sister's face, we were done for. That was hands-down one of my favorite performances ever! And easily one of our least professional.

{ Hailey }

A huge part of being able to find the humor in situations that maybe aren't so funny is learning to laugh at yourself! In a family like ours that loves to laugh, you are subject to being laughed at if you do something everyone else finds funny, so you can either choose to be offended and embarrassed and storm off or join in and all laugh together. As long as it's not mean spirited, letting your loved ones and friends help you laugh off your imperfect moments can help you not take yourself or life too seriously. Then you can have the confidence of Mandi and have the guts to say, with her, "If you spent ten seconds in my head, you would not BELIEVE how funny I am."

Yes, I did pull that gem from my family quotes on my phone.

{ Mandi }

I'm also grateful for the more character-building performance experiences we've had as sisters. Like the one time we all came off stage between long sets and started crying because we had just sung for an hour and not one soul had clapped or acknowledged us! Coffee shops are tough, man. As young girls, that experience was difficult in the moment, but now when we think about it, it makes us laugh just as hard as the others! Looking back, I wish I had laughed at that coffee shop instead of choosing to feel defeated.

Our experiences are what we make of them. I have learned one of the greatest joys of life is our ability to choose happiness in all the ups and downs of our experiences—especially those experienced together as sisters and family.

Creating loving family ties begins in the home, with YOU. Enjoy the time your family spends together, and intentionally give time and energy to strengthening your family bonds. Because of the example of our parents, we have learned that having a good sense of humor will help you build stronger sister ties.

Of course, no family is perfect. I repeat—no family is perfect! And ours is far from it. You may come from a family where your parents and siblings are not necessarily close, or you grew up in a house where you rarely said, "I love you," or "I miss you," and that's okay. As families and individuals, we go through a lot of hard things—but that's the point! We are put in our families to strengthen each other, to laugh together, to grow together, and to learn from each other.

Remember to laugh and smile when things get tough, or when relationships and experiences aren't perfect. Spend time together and allow yourself to love your family and siblings deeply. Whether you have strong bonds currently with your family or not, take the time to create memories and experiences with the people closest to you. You will look back on those forever and cherish them for the rest of your life.

I've learned that laughter can build bridges into the hearts of the people you love most, to connect you on a deeper level, and simply give you both something to smile about. Remember to choose to be happy, laugh with your family, and the people around you who feel like family, as much as you possibly can! It will keep life light, and it will open doors to having good, strong relationships with your siblings. For me, laughing together with my beautiful sisters over the years has made me realize that they truly are the greatest friends I could ever ask for. My sisters give me reason to smile. And that's part of what makes us sister strong.

Chapter 7

FRIENDSHIP

{ Mandi }

My sisters set the bar high when it comes to what I look for when choosing friends. My sisters truly are, even as my family members, my built-in best friends.

Hailey is someone I can always depend on. She always seems to have things together, and I know I can go to her for love and advice anytime I need it. Allie is always my comedic saving grace. She can get me laughing like no one, and I'm always feeling rejuvenated and less stressed when I'm around her. Lindsay is a calming force—very level headed with a touch of adventure. With Lindsay, I always know there will be good memories and good food no matter where we are or what we're doing. We always have a good time. When I'm around my sister Abby—oh man, that girl is hilarious! Her life is like a movie 24/7, and she seems to be a magnet for awkward and embarrassing moments that keep the entire family entertained. Despite her young age, I know I can always go to Abby for unconditional love and gospel-centered conversation. And then we have little Lucy. Lucy will totally throw you off because you'll swear you're staring at a ten-year-old, but you're having a conversation that you might have with a twenty-five-year-old. She's incredibly organized and can throw you a better birthday party than your peers, and she truly has the sweetest heart and most peaceful soul.

I feel blessed every day to have these women as my sisters— that I get to be around them daily and spend time getting to know the beautiful components that make up who they are. So with siblings like that, you could see why I often find it difficult to find friends who elevate me just as much as my sisters do, and who carry a strong, positive influence, but I too feel blessed in that area. I can honestly say my friends are also some of the greatest individuals I know.

One of the hardest but most rewarding things we can do with our time is find good friends. I've been thinking about common questions we ask ourselves when it comes to selecting the people we choose to keep close in our circle of influence. It is important to be mindful and thoughtful of a few things before investing in another person. Entrepreneur Jim Rohn stated, "You are the average of the five people you spend the most time with." With that being said, we know it's important to surround ourselves with people who inspire us to be better and motivate us to reach our potential. In the end, we become just like them, so we have to make our friendships count! When you surround yourself with individuals who inspire you to be the best version of you, you will know how effortless it is to want to do the same for others.

I've compiled a list of questions for this chapter that I have asked myself over and over again when navigating the friend department in life, as well as questions I often hear my peers are concerned about. With the hope that some of my personal experiences and wisdom of other church leaders and friends will help answer some of your questions around choosing the right friends, let's dive into what we know about good friendship:

How do I choose good friends?

I think one of the easiest ways to choose a good friend is to find out what's important to them. If your values and priorities line up with theirs, you are automatically going to be drawn to that person, simply because you both care about the same things.

One of my best friends gave me marriage advice that I think applies just as well to friendship. She told me to marry someone who is similar to me. Her reasoning made me laugh: "If you hate rock climbing and your spouse loves it, you're not going to have a whole lot of fun together having to do things you don't actually enjoy all the time. It's better to both like majority of the same things, so you can spend quality time together and have fun while you do it!" As it goes with friendships, finding friends who have the same values and even interests as you will help you bond and maintain your standards and priorities for your life. And of course you're not going to find your exact clone. There will always be things you do and like that are different from your friends, but as long as your ideals match up, you'll find you have a healthy balance of fun and growth when you're around your select group of people.

How do I know if my friend is someone I can trust?

As Hailey and I like to say, "Always trust a foodie." Though that is legitimately something we look to share with our friends, we know it can sometimes be difficult to decide who to become close to when navigating friendships.

Unfortunately, there's more to it than just finding another foodie. Although that is a good place to start. Just as choosing a good friend is essential, making sure your friend is someone you can trust is equally as important. In my life, I feel like I am friends with a lot of people. I really value being surrounded by people of different cultures and backgrounds and who know about topics I am not familiar with. I will say, however, that I have a select group of people I consider to be my friends.

These few people I know are trustworthy. They are good listeners and examples, and they are supportive of me. These are the few people I really open up to and share things with that I hold close to my heart. I think for a long time I was too nervous around my friends to be vulnerable and allow them to know a lot about my life. I feared that someone would use information against me or that I would get close to someone just for them to stop being friends with me eventually. I worried people only wanted to get to know me to boost Instagram followers or get to another sister. These were real but a bit irrational fears, and after some trial and error I realized a trick to knowing when and who to be open with—it's all based from a scripture that reads, "Even so every good tree bringeth forth good fruit; but a corrupt tree bringeth forth evil fruit. . . . Wherefore by their fruits ye shall know them" (Matthew 7:17, 20).

The best way to know who someone truly is is to look at their works; what they do. This includes how they interact with their family, what they spend their time on, what they think about and aspire to be, and especially how they treat others. If you notice light, truth, and good works flow from this person, then you can know they are trustworthy.

I think about a friend of mine, who I also had the opportunity to work with, who is a great example to me of this. She has been through a lifetime of difficulty, yet she is one of the most generous and brightest individuals I know! Not once did I ever hear her complain when work became difficult or when she was tired or going through a tough challenge. Better yet, it seemed that every time I was around her she was lifting someone else's spirits, including mine; lending a listening ear; taking care of someone who was struggling; driving people places; making food for someone else; or giving away her own things to people who needed it more. She consistently serves in church and frequently attends the temple. I often turn to this friend when I need advice or help, and without fail she is there to help me emotionally, spiritually, and physically. I am so grateful for her friendship in my life and the way she exemplifies selfless service.

Knowing that your friends are good people, by being blessed to be a part of the good works they omit, will be a strength to you. Uplifting and righteously proactive individuals are refreshing to be around, and like my friend does for me in my life, will inspire you to look outside of yourself and serve the people around you. Prayerfully seeking out these friends will bring joy and blessings as they add goodness to your life and peace to your soul because they are completely trustworthy individuals. If you haven't met a friend like this yet, try praying and asking Heavenly Father to put you in the path of an individual who is always doing good works. He will answer, and you will find good friends as you continue to strive to do the same.

How do I know if a friendship will last?

Growing up my family moved around quite a bit. Our mom loves change and has a gypsy heart, so we frequently moved homes, schools, and states throughout our younger years. It was rare for us to stay at the same school for more than a year, and making friends was always a difficult task. I never liked being "the new girl" and often dreaded the first day of school—especially if it meant coming into a new environment halfway through the year.

True almost everywhere, kids had their groups of friends usually with the same people they had grown up with since birth.

Every move I would pray long and hard to find at least one person I could connect with—especially on my first day at a new school.

In some places, that good friend would come right away, and in others it took weeks or months to bump into someone I really clicked with. There were even the schools where I literally had no friends the entire year, but I eventually found good people at church or in the neighborhood. Interestingly enough, I have at least one or two friends from every school, every state, and every place that we lived in who I *still* keep in touch with and love visiting when I get the chance! I know these friends will stay close to me for the rest of my life.

So how do you tell those individuals apart from the ones who seem to fade and change over time? Let me describe these friends to you and the qualities that make for lasting friendships:

The Preschool Bestie: This is my one friend who I have known literally my entire life. Probably even before that because our parents grew up together. I literally cannot remember life without her, and I just love her to pieces! I have learned from this friendship the importance of genuine caring. She is one of the best examples to me of a friend who remembers the important things, no matter how close or far apart we are. Every year since I can remember, this friend is either at my birthday celebrations or sending me some kind of message from wherever she is in the world at that time. She calls frequently and has for years. When we lived just a few doors down from each other during some of my middle school and high school years, she would show up at my house and talk with me about life and the good and bad I was facing each day. She has taught me more about taking the time to be a good friend than probably anyone else in my life—and she has done it since we were both young girls.

Because she is so great at keeping up with me despite distance, I feel like we have grown and changed together, and it has kept us close over the years. When we have the opportunity to be together, it is so easy to jump back into conversations like no time has passed. We enjoy each other's company because it really feels like we never left! She holds the bar high for me when it comes to what it looks like to be an involved friend. Her friendship is steady in my life, and I can't wait to see what else the future holds for her and how it will grow us even closer as we change and experience new things. My preschool bestie has demonstrated the positive impact genuine love will have on friendships.

The Elementary Soulmate: Goodness, I love this girl. Growing up in Washington together, we were in the same school and dance classes for years, and we pretty much lived at each other's houses on the weekends. I remember always laughing with this friend, and she fit right in with the rest of my siblings. We were just goofy kids—she came with all the crazy voices and accents and is one of the happiest people I know. Her energy has always been so refreshing, and despite how we have grown and what phase of life we find ourselves in next, she has stayed the same funny, sweet person she has always been. When I visit with her or we catch up over the phone, I leave feeling like my spirits have been lifted and I'm back to my carefree fourth-grade self. She is simply a good person. Anytime we're near each other, we try to meet up. It's been fun over the years to get together and see what's new and where life has taken us. There's usually always good food and plenty of reminiscing during these occasions. My elementary buddy taught me, even from a young age, to stay positive and keep positive individuals close to me.

The High School Homies: I was really blessed to stay in one state for the entirety of my Junior and Senior years of high school. There I was able to meet the nicest group of friends. We hung out all the time and would basically rotate houses every weekend just to make cookies, although my parents had second thoughts when my friend Ange and I blew up our brand-new oven. This sister-like bond in our group of friends was a great strength and confidence builder for me. All of us belonged to different faiths. I learned great life lessons from each of my friends in this group, and we all became very close. For me, it was a pivotal time in my life when being surrounded by so many good Christian girls helped me shape my values and stay true to my standards. These friends were uplifting, valued purity, and loved God. We had great religious conversations, and I always felt strengthened and turned toward Christ when interacting with them, and we had a special connection because of it. I know that is a rare find in high school, but I will always treasure that group of friends for the way they pushed me to be better during my teenage years. Maintaining friends who love God will empower your own progress and relationship with Him as well.

The College Crew: College friends were a hit-or-miss for me each semester as I navigated surrounding myself with good people. Most individuals I ran into were nice and outgoing, but I definitely found my fair share of flaky friends. I learned to stay away from friendships that involved any kind of arguing or disagreement, situations that made me feel out of place and uncomfortable, and personalities that brought out the worst in me. I learned that it's okay to be selective about your inner circle of influence—to spend time with and invest in other people who uplift and bring out your best self.

After selecting my close friends with intention and time, I am now able to look at the women around me with more gratitude than before. I honestly can't believe I found so many incredible individuals in one place while in college. The common trait I have noticed in this group of friends is that they are all incredibly bright. I mean that intellectually, spiritually, emotionally, socially, and physically, these girls glow! And every single one of them spreads that light to anyone they associate with. I feel incredibly blessed to be surrounded by friends like that, and I am grateful to have each one of them to look up to. My college crew has helped me recognize that lasting friendships are built on encouraging one another and having pure love and concern for each other's needs.

Friendships that will last consist of genuine care and pure joy. They are centered on Christ and are full of light and love. Any relationship that doesn't promote those things will inevitably grow dim and distant and will fail to add to your life and overall happiness. Friends are meant to bring you joy, so choose them wisely!

How can I be a better friend to others?

I recently had a dear friend of mine ask me after a heartfelt conversation, "What's one thing I can do to be a better friend to you?" Never before had anyone asked me that, and it both warmed my heart and threw me a little off guard because I wasn't sure how to answer. I was deeply touched that she would be concerned enough about me to want to help me where I needed it, and she cared enough about our friendship that she wanted to know how to improve it. I learned a great lesson that day about constantly improving my relationships with everyone in my life, including my friends.

I was inspired by the way my friend was able to look outward and make an open effort to make a great friendship even better. It was really humbling to me and has motivated me ever since to want to be more aware of how good of a friend I am being to others.

We don't have to necessarily have conversations with our friends to look for ways to develop better harmony with them. A great skill to develop is observation. Look for signs your friends may be struggling or discouraged, and then find ways to help serve them. Acting right away on ideas you have to better show your love and appreciation to your friends will bless both of your lives and grow you closer as you learn to appreciate each other more. Being aware of what's going on in the lives of your friends is also a great place to start. Give quality time to invest in the people you love, and both learn about them and from them. It's amazing how other's trials, upbringings, struggles, opinions, and views of the world can strengthen, inspire, and motivate you in your own life.

We are all here to learn from each other, and if you have that desire, get to know as much as you can about the people closest to you. You will find there is much to bond over, and you will find personal ways to make a difference in their lives based off what you know about them.

I'm a firm believer that friends are the sisters we get to choose for ourselves. One of the best friendships that exists in my life is a friendship that stemmed from randomly rooming with a girl while attending University in Utah. Upon meeting her, my life changed for the better. This sweet friend of mine is what I would call next-level caring. As roommates, we had many late-night conversations where we would start off telling jokes, then next we were having gospel conversations, and then all of a sudden, we'd flip into something serious, and then we'd be back to laughing. I've never had such a sister dynamic with a friend I've only known for a short amount of time. The greatest lesson I have learned from her is to allow compassion to guide your interactions within friendships. She has taught me that compassion in friendship will make all the difference in your dynamic and relationship and is an essential component to being a good friend to others.

I will never forget the first time I really felt this friend's pure love and compassion for me as we were sitting in the living room on our big brown couch having a heart-to-heart about anything and everything on our minds. At one point in our conversation I told my friend about a recent trip to Haiti I had been on and the way it had pulled at my heartstrings. It was still hard for me months later to think about because I wanted more than anything to still be in Haiti, and as I talked I got a little emotional thinking about the sweet kids I had interacted with and how much I missed them. I had been looking down, talking and thinking, and my friend got really quiet. When I finally looked up, I saw she had tears on her cheeks and pain in her eyes. I could feel she had complete empathy for everything I had been feeling, as if it were her own experience. She said nothing for a while, and we just cried together. I have had more moments similar to this one with her, where I have been hurting and she felt it with me. It is a spiritual gift that she can do that, and it's something that has brought feelings of great respect and gratitude for her for being there for me in such a sweet way.

When I am around her, I think of the Savior. That is exactly how I picture Him acting as a friend to the people He ministered to—and often to me as He assists me throughout my life. She truly has Christlike love for me, and all of her friends, as she is "willing to mourn with those that mourn; yea, and comfort those that stand in need of comfort, and to stand as witnesses of God at all times and in all things, and in all places" (Mosiah 18:9), and it makes her an incredible friend to many. By trying to do the same and praying for those qualities to help us be charitable and compassionate toward God's other children, we will come to be better friends to all those we associate with. What a blessing she has been in my life for allowing me to have the purest, sweetest connection to her that I will forever cherish and want to emulate. She has shown me what it is to be a true friend.

How do I maintain good friendships with my siblings?

Sometimes it can feel like it is the hardest to get along with our own family members verses friends outside sibling relationships. I try to remember to treat your friends like family, and your family like friends. But why can it be so difficult to get along better with your own siblings sometimes? My sibling relationships are far from perfect, but one thing I know for certain is that sibling relationships can be even greater than regular friendships if you allow them to be.

I understand that many may experience broken homes, complicated family situations, and even rough childhoods that all play factors into why sibling relationships may feel strained or distant. Some people have never been close to their siblings, because that's how it's been since childhood, and it may look daunting to try to start now. For those of you who find yourself in that situation, I would say don't stress about it. If you are prayerful with the Lord and have faith that one day good relationships are possible, you will come to have them. It will take effort, patience, and a whole lot of trial and error, but one thing is for sure—all things are possible with God. If you involve Him, it will be made clear what you should do and how to interact with each family member.

Relationships and friendships take effort. Coming from a large family with many different personalities, my sisters and I are all so different and can still get along. It's fascinating to me that we can grow up in the exact same environment, with the exact same parents, and have some of the exact same experiences, but end up so completely different from each other. That's sort of the beauty of families though. Differences take a little adaptation, but with the same ideas of love, kindness, compassion, empathy, service, and sacrifice, family members are the greatest friends you could ever ask for. The best part is, they don't come and go!

My family is forever. And I couldn't imagine it any other way. Each of my sisters and my two sweet brothers are all incredible people who have amazing talents and abilities and who teach me valuable lessons every single day. Of course we have our moments that aren't pretty where we argue and fight, but at the end of the day we know we can trust each other. I know my siblings will be honest with me, they will inspire me to try my best and be my best, and we are united in the gospel together—which is the greatest element to bond over. Our interactions become so much deeper than just a good memory or a fun time. We know that our relationships are eternal, and we want them to last forever and to be joyful.

If we fight, we try to fix things quickly. We know we need to mend things that have been hurt or broken because those relationships are worth it. They are irreplaceable and priceless. Having family members that you can count on and being a family member your siblings and parents can depend on will completely enrich your life and give you special perspective. Remembering that family relationships matter most will remind you to cherish and treat your family with deep respect and love. And because of your respect for them, it will be easy to remember to speak kindly to one another, to frequently express your love to your siblings, to cheer them on when they have success, and to cry with them when they need you to be there and be their friend.

Family and friends make life beautiful. We have them so we don't have to go through it alone. Let your siblings be more important than your things, your problems, your arguments, and your schedule. Allow your family members to be close to you. As Marvin J. Ashton expressed, "Yes, a friend is a person who is willing to take me the way I am but who is willing and able to leave me better than he found me."[1] Your family members are the people who are most qualified to do this. Love them and love them for it, and remember that they're the ones who will be with you for time and all eternity.

NOTE

1. Marvin J. Ashton, "What Is a Friend?" *Ensign,* Jan. 1973.

Chapter 8

BEING A PEACEMAKER

{ Hailey }

When I was a freshman in high school, we started taking voice lessons from a wonderful coach named Dan Truhitte. Dan is most well known for his role as Rolf and his iconic performance of the song "Sixteen Going on Seventeen" in the film *The Sound of Music.* He was such a sweet and encouraging mentor and helped all of us build confidence in our voices.

After a few months of lessons, Dan invited us to perform with him in a show for over a thousand veterans in a nearby city. We sang "Boogie Woogie Bugle Boy" to a warm, big crowd who clapped and sang along. We closed the show by singing a song called "Let There Be Peace on Earth" with Dan. I've never forgotten what it felt like to sing those words with the men and women who had sacrificed so much in the name of peace.

> Let there be peace on earth and let it begin with me.
> With God as our father,
> Brothers all are we.
> Let me walk with my brother in perfect harmony.[1]

Let's walk together in harmony, sisters! For us to experience peace in our relationships with each other, inner peace has to arise from within each of us.

Jesus Christ is the ultimate example of a peacemaker. He is the "Prince of Peace" (Isaiah 9:6). When we strive to follow and be like Him and impart peace to our fellow brothers and sisters, we can better live in harmony with one another.

We learn from many witnesses in scripture that our Savior was never reactive. No matter what was said or done to Him, He never lashed out in anger, argued, or stirred up contention among his brethren. "Charity suffereth long" (1 Corinthians 13:3), and our Lord was indeed long suffering. "Wherefore, they scourge him, and he suffereth it; and they smite him, and he suffereth it. Yea, they spit upon him, and he suffereth it, because of his loving kindness and his long-suffering toward the children of men" (1 Nephi 19:9).

With twenty-twenty hindsight, I can see how I at times contributed to a spirit of contention that made it difficult to have peace in our home of a family of ten.

Some of us—I won't point fingers—were known as the "pot-stirrers" and loved to add our two cents at very inopportune moments. A word of advice to all seeking for peace in your family: don't stir the pot. Don't even dip your little spoon in for a taste.

A favorite scripture of mine is 4 Nephi 1:15, which reads: "There was no contention in the land because of the love of God which did dwell in the hearts of the people."

President Russell M. Nelson expands on this scripture: "Thus, love of God should be our aim. It is the first commandment—the foundation of faith. As we develop love of God and of Christ, love of family and neighbor will naturally follow."[2]

If I'm honest, it has taken me a long time to put this into practice to be a peace builder. More often than not, I'm more like a disturber of the peace. But I've learned some valuable lessons about caring for my fellow sisters and how much of a difference it makes to have a peacemaker in your home.

When I moved away to attend college I assumed it would be easier to get along with people other than my siblings, but the challenge of maintaining peace in the home followed me wherever I went.

One set of roommates I lived with was messy and sloppy, and it drove this neat freak a little bit crazy. They left meals they had cooked out on the stovetop for days, stinking up our house, left trails of their long hair on every surface, and would somehow flood the bathroom, covering the floor with several inches of water every time they showered. And to top it all off, every Sunday, these roommates would invite tons of people over who would take over our house and leave it a complete disaster.

Do you see where this is headed? I'll give you a hint: it ain't no zen circle of sister trust and unity.

I wanted to host a dinner in our home for some of my coworkers, and I let my roommates know in advance I was having people over so they would have time to find somewhere else to enjoy their meal.

This is where things got ugly.

When the night of my planned dinner arrived, I came home from church to a house full of people, none of which were my coworkers.

As my friends started arriving, I had to squish them into a corner. I tried to cook in our small kitchen space, working around the other uninvited guests. My friends could clearly see what was happening, and everyone felt awkward the whole night.

Sister, let me tell you. I was beyond mad. In my mind, my roommates were the most inconsiderate girls I had ever met.

So naturally I handled things in a really mature, peacemaking manner.

I complained about them to my other friends and sisters, who validated my concerns and led me to feel justified in my dislike for them. The last thing I wanted to be toward them was civil and peaceful. I gave them fake smiles and avoided them at all costs, my resentment toward them constantly building every time I'd have to clean up their mess or nearly meet my death each time I'd step onto the wet bathroom floor.

It got to the point where the tension I felt every time I was around them started to make it hard to feel peace in our home. After a couple months of frustrating encounters, miscommunications, and misunderstandings, I decided I didn't want our home life to be full of tension and anger anymore. I decided I was going to try to be a peacemaker by loving and serving my roommates.

One afternoon shortly after I'd made this decision, I was on my hands and knees, scrubbing the kitchen floor clean. I was so excited, thinking my roommates would see the selfless act of love I was performing for all of us living in the house and we'd experience the magic of friendship like on *My Little Pony*!

I had just reached the last tile in the kitchen when one of my roommates walked in.

This is it! I thought to myself.

She said a quick hello and walked straight past me into the kitchen . . . leaving a trail of muddy footprints all over my freshly. Cleaned. Floor.

She didn't even notice what I was doing!

I sat on the floor on my knees and stared at her in disbelief. Then I stood up, walked to my bedroom, closed the door, and cried.

That was the moment I realized that I couldn't wait for them to change in order to feel peace. I had to find it on my own.

There is no magical happy ending to this story. We never became best friends. In fact, they moved out after just one semester, and I started fresh with new roommates that brought with them their own set of challenges. Though I tried my best to love and serve my roommates in ways that I thought were important, things didn't always go according to plan.

Even though my roommates didn't suddenly become organized and tidy, what truly mattered is that my heart changed. I learned that if I prayed for help from God, I could carry peace within myself, despite what others around me might choose to do.

I know that the Lord sees every small effort we make to be a peacemaker, even if it is not received in the way we hope.

A year later, I moved into a new house with a girl who didn't turn out to be the kind of friend I'd hoped for. Her true colors were revealed pretty quickly after I moved in, and I didn't trust her. The Lord blessed us with another amazing roommate, Chelsea, who acted as the peacemaker in our home.

When we weren't getting along great, Chelsea eased the tension, invited us to fun activities, wrote us notes, put her arms around us, talked with us, and baked us cookies. She brought us both closer to Christ and allowed us to live in harmony with each other. We had peace in our home, despite our differences. Her friendship is one that I deeply value, and she is someone that I still look up to and admire today.

Chelsea was able to see the good in both our roommate and myself and love us both equally despite our imperfections and quirks. She brought her own sense of inner peace to our home, and her example was what made all the difference. She chose to act exactly how I'd imagine our Savior would: putting His arm around us, ministering to us individually, and helping us see the good in each other.

Only God can give us the kind of peace that is lasting, that enables us to speak softly, to act with kindness, to avoid fighting and arguing with each other or letting our differences come between us. Jesus Christ's reassuring promise can fill us with His love and a sense of peace: "Peace I leave with you, my peace I give unto you: not as the world giveth, give I unto you" (John 14:27).

We must be at peace with ourselves in order to promote peace in our families, homes, and communities. The key to having peace and avoiding contention is to have our hearts filled with the love of God. Only God can give us the kind of peace that is lasting, that enables us to speak softly, to act with kindness, to avoid fighting and arguing with each other or letting our differences come between us. When we carry this peace in each of our hearts, we can be peacemakers to our sisters and better live in harmony.

{ Mandi }

Like Hailey, I too have had my moments of disrupted peace. One was on a recent internship on a small island in Tonga. I had just come off a week teaching English to students from the ages of eight to eighteen at a local Christian school. These kids were incredibly humble and receptive to learning. Most days the school couldn't afford to pay its teachers, so many of the classrooms would be filled to the brim with eager students and no instructor. I would go from class to class, between all the age groups as the day progressed, and stand in for an hour at a time to teach.

Each time I walked into a classroom, no matter the age of the students, they would stand and greet me, smiling ear to ear. We accomplished much learning in the few short weeks I was there, and the time came for me to be transferred to the church school down the street. On my first day, I expected it to be just like my experience at the Christian school, but within the first class period I realized that would not be the case.

A rowdy group of teenage boys found it entertaining to make my lesson comical, and as a foreigner half their size, I didn't stand a chance trying to discipline them. I tried my best to ignore the snickers, the sly comments in a language I couldn't understand that would make the other kids giggle, and the ongoing musical chairs that would happen every time I turned my back to write on the board. For the first time in years, I felt like I was about to lose my cool!

The class period ended, and I tried to continue with my work-day, but my blood was boiling. I lived on the school's campus, and my room was a short walk from my classroom, so I was able to go home for my lunch break. I came storming through the door to see my roommate (who happens to also be one of my best friends), who I thought would be gone whale watching all day, sitting at the kitchen table. I immediately started to tell her about this group of students who tried so hard to ruin my lesson and who I almost let ruin my day.

Maybe it was the heat of the islands that afternoon or the flame we had to rig to get our stove to turn on—we'll never know—but I took a quick breather in my room, and all of a sudden, it hit me! I was about to do something insane. I came running back out to the kitchen, took one look at my room-mate, and said, "This is crazy, but I have this idea . . ." When she responded, "You know I support your crazy ideas," we were already halfway out the door to the school's principal's office.

Call it destiny, but as we entered the office we learned the principal was sick, and any request would need to be made to the vice principal. I don't even remember her looking up from her computer as I requested to take three students off campus for the lunch period. Upon her green light, we were running back to my classroom to search the school's system for student names.

If I were a detective, this would've been the peak of my career. I found the attendance for that period and asked the regular teacher to try to recall the names of the kids that sat in the seats I needed. You better believe we got those names!

With no time to lose, I began running up to groups of students eating lunch to ask if they knew the kids I was looking for based off of the list of names I had. Within minutes, we located them. Determined to get through to these three disruptive students, we half begged one of the staff members to start up the school bus (for like fifteen people) to drive the five of us a few feet down the road to the Christian school. We stormed into a classroom with one of my favorite groups of students and asked the teacher if we could borrow his class for just a few minutes. He readily agreed and stepped out. Thinking this was the only way I was going to teach these kids a lesson, I set three chairs up in front of the other students and began lecturing them on how they should be more like the kids in front of them at this Christian school.

Just as I felt like I had said my piece and like my demonstration had shown these students that they needed to respect others, especially me as their teacher, the biggest trouble maker of the group chimed in with one final sassy comment. My mouth dropped and eyes went wide. All I could think of was, "Oh no he did not!" and before I could let another word out, my roommate called him outside to deal with him personally.

I tried to gather my thoughts, worried that there was nothing I could do to show these students I wanted to help them succeed, and I tried to continue with my speech on respect and Christianity. Exhausted, I stopped talking and turned to look at the humble students behind me that I had enjoyed teaching just a few days before. One of my most soft-spoken and hard-working students in the corner raised her hand and said, "Ms. G? Do you think I could talk to them?" Thrown off, I responded, "Oh. Well yes, of course." She then gave me the sweetest, most understanding look and half whispered, "If it's all right with you, I would like to do it in our native language." I nodded in approval and sat down, feeling defeated, in my chair.

She stood at her desk and began speaking to the remaining students seated behind me in a calm, soft voice. Her eyes were bright but determined as she spoke. I had no idea what she was saying to the other students, but it didn't matter—whatever it was completely transformed the entire atmosphere in the room. I felt the students relax in their chairs and my shoulders even soften. A peaceful spirit filled the room. When she finished and sat down, we were all smiling. I was filled with relief at her loving example in trying to help me communicate to the other students, and I knew it was the perfect time to try to establish that mutual respect I was hoping for.

Naturally, I grabbed my candy bag from my backpack, and handed it to my former student to grab some first and pass it around the room. She accepted the candy, smiled with her head down, got up from her desk, and walked past me to the students I had been getting in trouble.

They felt bad accepting and politely pushed it away, saying things like, "No it's okay," and "We shouldn't," but she persisted with comments like, "Then take some for your friends . . . your siblings . . . just go ahead." When she knew they weren't going to accept it, in front of the entire class, she knelt down on the filthy, dust-covered ground at the student's feet. With the bag extended, she whispered, "Please. We all want you to take some first."

The room went silent. Peace filled my heart. She stayed there until they slowly accepted. I had to look away. I had tears in my eyes, for truly in that moment I had been taught the greatest lesson of all. It takes humility to be a true peacemaker. Trying to elicit mutual respect and love for others cannot be born in the heat of anger, but instead in the arms of love and meekness.

That afternoon, my sweet student taught me something I will never forget: what it looks like to spread peace and understanding the way the Savior would. Problems cannot be solved with harsh words or prideful hearts. Through her example, I saw firsthand the effectiveness of a soft answer and a loving act of kindness. I will never forget that experience and the humility she demonstrated. As we follow the example of this incredible young woman and the example of our Savior, Jesus Christ, we will be able to spread love and understanding more effectively to all the sisters around us—no matter where we are in the world or what our circumstances may be.

Notes

1. Sy Miller and Jill Jackson, "Let There Be Peace on Earth," Beverly Hills, CA: Jan-Lee Music, 1972.
2. Russell M. Nelson, "The Canker of Contention," *Ensign*, May 1989.

Chapter 9

MAYBE IT'S ME

{ Hailey }

A man very dear to us and his wife had planned to come visit our family while we were living in North Carolina. The day of the trip arrived, and before heading to the airport, the man took their dog for a walk. The dog meandered around and did her business, and he cleaned it up immediately like the good neighbor that he was. The couple headed to the airport, made their way through security, and boarded their flight.

As soon they were seated on the plane, the man noticed an unpleasant smell that seemed to be coming from the other passenger seated on their row.

Phew! he thought. *What is that smell?*

He assumed their seat neighbor must not have been feeling well and leaned as far away as he could from the other man as the plane took off into the sky. The smell lingered in the air circulating through the plane as they flew several hours to North Carolina. By the time they landed, the stink was almost more than the man could bear. They quickly gathered their bags and stepped out into the airport, but the smell appeared to follow them wherever they went.

Sheesh! the man thought. *This airport smells awful too!*

The smell continued to follow the couple into their rental car, throughout their drive, and all the way up to their hotel room.

"This whole state smells horrible!" the man said out loud to himself.

As the couple settled into their hotel room, the man checked his shoes. He checked his wife's shoes. Then the man reached into his jacket pocket and discovered something quite unpleasant.

The little doggie bag from his morning walk had traveled all the way to North Carolina with him.

It hadn't been the man sitting next to him on the plane, the airport, or the entire state of North Carolina that had stunk to high heaven. It had been the little gift he himself had forgotten he'd put in his own jacket pocket.

How often do we go through life blaming others for the poor relationships, problems, and inconveniences we endure? Sometimes we act like the entire world is working against us, as if everything unpleasant that happens to us is everyone else's fault. We say things like "What's their problem?" or "I didn't do anything and she was still so mean to me," or "It wasn't my fault," or "Who does she think she is?"

Perhaps we should start asking ourselves a new question:

What if it's me?

What if I'm part of the problem?

Sister, you are in complete control of how you view others and the world around you.

When things feel off in your relationships, maybe part of the problem is you.

As the oldest children in a large family, our parents emphasized the importance of setting a good example for our younger siblings from the time we were old enough to understand that they were watching and emulating everything we did. Our mom would constantly cut into conversations amongst the older kids by saying, "You have little ears listening!" or "They're soaking in everything you do and say like a sponge."

By no means were we perfect examples for each other; we fought, argued, shouted, called each other names, and snuck into each other's rooms to eat each other's stashes of candy (Mandi never lets me forget that one) all the time. But the principle of taking responsibility for our own actions is one that we've carried into our adult lives, and this has helped us navigate through difficult times in our relationships within our family and even with our friends.

When relationships are strained, I've found that ruminating and dwelling on the faults of others never leads to healing and change. Withholding love or friendship until the other person admits fault, apologizes, or suddenly becomes who you would like them to be is just like assuming the unpleasant smell is coming from everyone else. Well, sis, maybe it's not. Maybe you're part of the problem, too!

I'll let you in on a little secret that could transform the relationships in your life:

The only person you have control over is *you*.

Relationship struggles can be seen with fresh eyes when we take a step back and ask the Lord to help us see where we might be contributing to the problem. Of course boundaries have to be put into place where abusive, toxic, or manipulative relationships are only tolerable at a great distance or, in some cases, when cut off completely, if that's what's necessary for your safety. But if we're honest with ourselves, in most relationship issues it's possible to see where we might be contributing to the problem.

It's good for me to regularly assess what's working, what's not working, what I actually have control over, and what I may be able to do to change or improve things in my family relationships. What I've learned is that the only thing *I* have control over is how I see and feel about the people around me. I have absolutely no control over how they see or feel about me, and there is nothing I can do to force someone else to change how they see or feel about me. There is simply nothing we can do to change another person, how they see us, or how they feel about us.

Dieter F. Uchtdorf gave an amazing talk entitled "Three Sisters" in which he discussed this principle of taking responsibility for our own discipleship:

> What did the Savior teach? "I say unto you, Love your enemies, bless them that curse you, do good to them that hate you, and pray for them which despitefully use you, and persecute you; That ye may be the children of your Father which is in heaven." This is the Savior's way. It is the first step in breaking down the barriers that create so much anger, hatred, division, and violence in the world.
>
> "Yes," you might say, "I would be willing to love my enemies—if only they were willing to do the same." But that doesn't really matter, does it? We are responsible for our own discipleship, and it has little—if anything—to do with the way others treat us. We obviously hope that they will be understanding and charitable in return, but our love for *them* is independent of their feelings toward *us*.
>
> Perhaps our effort to love our enemies will soften their hearts and influence them for good. Perhaps it will not. But that does not change our commitment to follow Jesus Christ.[1]

Is it possible to love others who do not love us? Absolutely. Is it extremely difficult at times? Yes ma'am, it is!

God works with me to maintain many "one-sided" relationships in my life as I strive to obey the Lord's commandment to love as He loves us, without expecting anything in return. It is not easy to invest in someone who may not return the affection, attention, or effort you give them, but most of what I've felt for those people isn't something that they can give me or something I can muster up on my own.

God knows the ins and outs of their hearts; He knows everything about them, the good, the bad, and the ugly, and still loves them perfectly. He sees the unkind deeds they may have done to us, as well as those we may inflict on others. All of us are imperfect and yet are all deserving and worthy of love. But that doesn't mean we have to summon up some kind of magical fairytale love for everyone around us by ourselves.

We can't love everyone perfectly on our own! We need God's help. Because He knows and loves each of us perfectly, our Heavenly Father can impart a portion of His love for them in our hearts, allowing us to be free from hurt and sorrow and enabling us to forgive, forget, and move forward.

As one of my favorite artists, Lauren Aquilina, sings in her song "Broke," sometimes "those hardest to love need it most."[2]

I had an experience where I felt like it was impossible for me to forgive and love some particular people in my life.

I was praying daily, sometimes hourly, for God to take away my hurt feelings and anger that flared up all the time. I couldn't even participate in conversations about them without feeling horribly wronged as I relived their unkind words and actions toward my family and me over and over. I tried and failed to understand what any of us had done to deserve it, feeling that I was completely justified in being upset with them, telling myself that anyone would be if they had been in my shoes and been wronged as I had. I was waiting for them to own up to their wrongs, apologize, and make things right, all while sinking deep into a hole of resentment and sorrow.

After many months of heartache and wrestling with this issue, I sat in yet another quiet moment of prayer alone and asked my Heavenly Father fervently, for what felt like the thousandth time, to be relieved from my resentful feelings. As entitled as I felt to my inability to forgive quickly, I knew I was being so prideful! I was so tired of feeling hurt and upset about what had happened and wanted to be completely free of the burdens I was carrying. A very clear impression came into my mind through the Spirit:

You're never going to be able to move on from this until you decide to let go completely and not look back.

I sat still and thought about the words I had felt in my mind. Peace settled over my heart, and I knew it was the piece of my puzzle that I hadn't been able to place up until that point. To truly let go and move on, I had to turn away from everything that had happened, leave it behind me, fix my eyes on Jesus Christ, and choose not to look back again.

I knew He could lead me out of this as He had many times before but hadn't realized that the real root of the problem was *me*. I was holding *myself* back from accessing His grace by constantly dwelling on and reliving the past. Jesus Christ was the only way I could experience healing and lasting peace, and it required surrendering all of it, everything I had been holding on to, and laying it at His feet.

I chose to act on that inspiration and tried my best to let it all go. Though I experienced great peace in that moment of prayer and revelation, I had to fight to maintain peace, and the hard feelings I had harbored for so long did not disappear all at once for me.

And you know what else? Those people have not changed one bit. They never apologized or owned up to their actions or did anything that *I* thought they should do. When the temptation arises to think about the hard moments of the past, I have to let those thoughts go and remember where I stand with that person or group of people *right now*. Our circumstances haven't changed much, but my heart and paradigm changed, and I was freed up and empowered to do my part to make things right.

To my surprise, it was my feelings that actually changed, and our relationships have started to improve over time.

From that experience, I learned that lasting forgiveness is only possible when we ask God to work a change in our own hearts, not waiting for other people to change first. Healing is possible through Jesus Christ, whose grace allows each of us to be responsible for our own discipleship. Though we can't change anyone else, we can lay our broken hearts at His feet over and over, and He will equip us with new insights and perspectives about others that we can't see on our own.

He is the one who gives us the strength to eventually move on. I know that through the enabling power of the Atonement of Jesus Christ, it is possible for us to drop our pride and to love the unlovable and forgive the unforgivable. What a miracle!

Choosing to follow in the Savior's way gives others space to be themselves and to use their own agency to love and embrace those around them at their own pace while empowering us to take responsibility for the quality of our relationships in our own hearts.

Notes

1. Dieter F. Uchtdorf, "Three Sisters," *Ensign*, Nov. 2017, 16–20.
2. Lauren Aquilina, "Broke," *Liars*, 2014.

Chapter 10

BEING THE ONLY ONE

{ Hailey }

During my final semester of college, Allie, Mandi, and I got jobs bussing tables at a massive buffet-style restaurant that catered to thousands of tourists every night. It was hard work! We had to cart around trays with bins stacked full of hundreds of dirty cups, plates, and utensils; keep the guests happy and cater to their diet or culture specific meal requests; and maintain order in a potentially chaotic environment.

After the last guest would leave the restaurant, we'd have a few minutes to make a plate of food for ourselves and then a few more minutes to shovel it down before doing our closing work assignments and heading home. Despite the busyness of the job, we worked hard and tried to make the most of it. We became great friends with many hard-working and hilarious students from all over the world.

The most challenging part about this job was the work environment itself. Our boss, in the words of Nacho Libre, was a *"CRAZY LADY."* She had a really strict policy around our uniform, hairstyle, and lipstick colors but didn't emphasize anything to do with work ethic. She would say really unkind, condescending things to try to motivate us in our work, which created a stressful, disharmonious environment.

{ Mandi }

I'm pretty sure I have an unfinished six-page letter to that restaurant somewhere speaking my mind. I probably should've sent it years ago. Oh well. It turned out to be a great bonding moment for us as sisters, and it's something we laugh a lot about now, even if it wasn't that funny in the moment.

{ Hailey }

While most of us were picking chicken bones and used tissues out of cloth napkins and mopping floors, a few employees and managers that our boss favored could usually be found lounging in the back of the kitchen, sneaking cake from the fridge. They avoided work while everyone else ran around like crazy. The rest of us joked about how if one of us dared to be that openly lazy, she'd fire us on the spot.

{ Mandi }

I totally remember how one of them managed to flood the floor of the kitchen one night, and before we could warn Hailey, who, bless her heart, was trying to get food quickly out to the customers, she took a false step and slid across the floor—arms flailing and hair flying—falling straight on her back! I remember our co-worker who we loved so much screaming, "HAILEY! NOOO!"

and all of us laughing as we tried to help her off the floor! Good times, good times.

{ Hailey }

Oh, heavens. I'd forgotten about that little episode! I shall add it to my mental file folder of embarrassing falls.

Anyway, at different points in our lives, we've encountered a few women who try to split us up or separate us from each other, as if they think it's their job to break up our sisterhood or help us befriend others. This boss was one of those people.

Allie and I were asked to become "serenaders," going from table to table singing to people celebrating special occasions, while Mandi continued to bus tables and had to watch us sing without her. It was a total Cinderella and the ugly stepsisters situation!

One day after a few months of working at the restaurant, I came to work without having time to slick my hair back into a perfect bun. I felt her eyes on me immediately after clocking in. Sure enough, she approached me as I was preparing the restaurant for opening and told me she wanted to talk. She took me back to an empty corner of the kitchen, where no one else was in sight, and said to me, "Your hair isn't right. I'm going to have to send you home."

{ Mandi }

Allie and I had been assigned to work up front that day, and I just so happened to walk to the back to switch my bin out (yes, I was bussing tables while my sisters sang jingles) just as the door to the stairway swung closed, and I caught a glimpse of what looked like Hailey cornered by our boss. So I did what any sister would do, and I dropped my bin on a cart and went running out to Allie. All I had to say was, "She's got Hailey cornered!" and we were both flying to the back stairway!

{ Hailey }

Meanwhile, I stared at our boss in disbelief. As far as I knew, she'd never sent any of the others girls home because their hair wasn't styled right! I needed every dollar I could get to pay for school and rent, and couldn't believe I was about to get an entire shift taken off my paycheck. I felt singled out and threatened.

So naturally I totally kept my cool.

"Are you serious?" I said. "There are like five other girls out there whose hair looks just like mine. Why aren't you talking to all of us? Why aren't you sending them home?"

She avoided eye contact with me and for once didn't have anything to say. I was so tired of her intimidation tactics. So I quit! Right there on the spot.

"Fine. Come fill out your paperwork," she said as she started heading up the stairs to her office.

I stomped up the stairs behind her.

Suddenly, like a movie, Allie and Mandi came bursting through the door to the kitchen. They had seen our boss corner me and knew something was up.

{ Mandi }

Allie and I came running to what we thought would be to the rescue—what we were planning on doing when we got there, I have no idea—but when we opened the door all I saw was the tail of Hailey's creepy green muumuu sweep around the corner out of sight. Before Hailey caught our faces, I'm pretty sure I let out a little giggle, and was like, "Uhh, Hailey?" and then she said the magic words, and we knew we were destined to go down together. In style, of course.

{ Hailey }

I'm pretty sure my muumuu was a really obnoxious shade of pink, but yes, it was indeed creepy.

"What's happening?" Mandi asked, concerned.

"I JUST QUIT!" I yelled back at her down the stairs.

I turned around and saw them look at each other determinedly.

{ Mandi }

"Well then, so do we!" I said.

Sometimes it takes a little bit for things to blow over for them to become funny eventually. Yeah, that was not one of those times. It was funny right away.

{ Hailey }

Allie and Mandi followed me up the stairs into our boss's office, where she sat at her computer, refusing to look at any of us as we each signed our notices and then left the restaurant together.

Without hesitation, they were by my side in a tough moment when I felt singled out and alone. Even though I thought I'd be the only one walking home jobless that night, my sisters were also unemployed, thanks to my decision to quit. You know what they say: a family that quits together, stays together.

I'll admit, if I had humbled myself and fixed my hair the way I was supposed to, I might have avoided this confrontation all together. I definitely could have handled things in a more mature, harmonious manner and tried to find a way to connect with my boss despite our differences. Though I've since learned from my mistakes, I'm glad we have such a dramatic and funny story to tell all these years later!

Toward the end of my high school years, I worked at a movie theater in Southern California. It was my first experience working in customer service, and I made countless mistakes but learned a lot about treating people (especially angry people) with kindness and respect and being hard working and dependable.

I did have a few memorable and unpleasant episodes, like when I was asked to refill the huge ice bin and rolled it into its slot in the concessions area, not knowing it was backward, flooding the floor with melting ice water instead of sending it down the drain. We all had wet shoes and had to slosh through water for the rest of the night because of me.

And then there was the time I accidentally pushed the wrong button on the nacho cheese machine and hot, bright orange cheese continued pouring out of the spout even after my little cup was full. I scrambled for something else to catch it with, covering my hands and my uniform in the nuclear stuff.

One of my coworkers (who happened to be a boy—a cute boy) walked by right at that moment, looked me up and down, and said, "You would."

Very validating.

Most of my shifts were during the day, and movie theaters are pretty much empty before 5:00 p.m., so I spent a lot of time talking with and getting to know my coworkers. The guys I worked with in concessions and the box office became good friends of mine. We laughed and had so much fun together, finding ways to keep ourselves entertained as we worked, and I got pretty good at making popcorn under the tutelage of my friend George.

I remember I was asked to work in a different area one day and was assigned to clean theaters with a girl I hadn't really talked to before. After our manager explained our tasks to us, I responded with a smile and went to work cleaning, not knowing that my co-worker was watching me.

She approached me in the dim lights of one of the theaters we were cleaning and asked, "Are you high?"

I was caught completely off guard. "What? No, of course not."

"You're totally high," she insisted.

"I don't do drugs," I replied.

She laughed at me rudely and refused to believe that I wasn't on drugs and that I had never touched drugs or alcohol. She then said something I've never forgotten.

"Well, whatever you're on, I want some of it. Nobody is *that* happy."

As she walked away, I'll admit I was totally offended at her insistence of something that was completely false, but that afternoon I thought a lot about what she had said and began to develop pity for her. It made me sad that she couldn't believe that I had always chosen to stay away from harmful substances and that someone could be as happy as I was cleaning movie theaters without the help of some kind of drug to make it bearable.

As a Christian girl in a high school environment full of peers experimenting with drugs, alcohol, and immoral behavior, I certainly felt at times that I was all alone in my sobriety and moral standards. Being someone who *wasn't* doing those things was so rare that it was nearly impossible for my co-worker to believe. But, clearly, it made me stand out. My ability to smile and sweep, or make mistakes and shrug them off, or choose not to participate in talking badly about others made me different.

Being the only one means choosing to be different, choosing to go against the grain.

Different is being the only girl wearing a modest prom dress at the school dance or the only girl on the entire island who always wears a one-piece swimsuit and has never owned a bikini. Different is saying no when everyone else is saying yes. Different is helping the mom whose child spills in the grocery store when everyone else just stares at her or walks by. Different is empowering. Different is choosing not to watch popular movies or TV shows or read best-selling books even though all your friends do because some of their content doesn't align with your values.

Different is so good.

Since that time, I've been able to find wonderful friends who share my same values but are still different from me in good ways. It's so empowering to finally feel connected to other women who feel like my long-lost sisters, who share similar interests, and who make me realize that there were other girls like me living out in the world all along. Women who were different from everybody else, just like I was. Women I just hadn't had the chance to meet yet.

Being the only one looks like being different but feels like knowing who you truly are and what you value most. Being different builds strength of character and resilience in your beliefs and values as you practice them. I don't know what came of that girl from the movie theater, but I hope that she found her happiness in something that will last. My happiness comes from living a life that often requires me to stand on my own and sometimes be the only one. And I know that it really is possible to be *that* happy by living the principles of the gospel of Jesus Christ, because with Him, we are never alone.

{ Mandi }

Before we moved to North Carolina, my family and I spent four years in beautiful Washington State. We lived near Seattle, where the weather is cozy, nature is stunning, and people gather from around the world. It's one of my favorite places we ever lived and is still one of my favorite places to visit. We grew up attending colorful Indian weddings and smelling the luring spices of curry from the kitchen of our next-door neighbors. We learned in school of the richness of Native American culture and of different traditions from societies around the globe.

We spent most of our time outdoors and enjoyed the weekends in Canada with our grandparents. I always looked forward to our visits to Vancouver where I learned to love ethnic foods at a young age. I think my love for Asian cultures began there and is probably the reason why I love Japanese cuisine and Korean traditions. Living in Washington was a rich cultural experience for me as a kid, so when our dad's job took him to North Carolina, we were in for a bit of a shock.

Let's just say things were done differently there. "Southern Culture" wasn't a bad thing, but it did take a bit of adjusting to get used to. My experience turned more into learning how to fry everything you eat, stick to what you know, and stay where you're at. Good things can come from this mindset, like valuing family time and closeness, and I loved the Christian community in the South. You could actually tell someone, "Merry Christmas" in school, unlike in Washington, but I definitely was grateful for the way Washington opened my mind and allowed me to embrace other people and their traditions.

High school in North Carolina was completely different from the other places we had previously lived. With both Washington and California to compare to, sometimes I felt the mindset of my peers to be somewhat limiting and maybe even a little sheltered at times.

My early high school years involved moving back and forth from North Carolina and California quite a bit; this was the beginning of a busy stage of music for our family. We had work opportunities and goals we were pursuing with singing and acting, and so we would spend part of the year traveling to work on those things. This was around the same time we started our YouTube channel. We couldn't believe people were actually watching our videos, and with just a couple hundred followers, we began taking cover requests. YouTube still astounds me to this day because of how someone on the other side of the world can watch your art and feel connected to you.

We received a request from a young girl to cover a K-pop song (which we didn't even realize existed), and of course the song was one we had never heard of. I remember me, Hailey, and Allie crowding around the computer screen to look it up. Needless to say, that request changed our world—our poor dad. We all got into K-pop because of it. The music and videos were like nothing we had ever seen before. I fell in love with the culture a little bit more than the rest of my sisters, though we all appreciated the artists and music made in Korea.

I became fascinated with the culture, food, people, music, pop culture, and language. Our dad, though he didn't completely understand the obsession, even took us to The Hollywood Bowl for a K-pop festival, where we were one of the few non-Korean families there. It was amazing and pretty comical. I'm grateful for my dad's love of travel and culture because he introduced us at a young age to cultures from around the world, and it has enriched my life experience. With parents who love travel and culture, especially global cuisine, I can't help but love being around people from different places in the world. Coming from experiences and teenage phases like my Korean one (which I'm not sure I completely got out of) back to slow and steady, don't-do-anything-different North Carolina, was a hard adjustment.

I'll never forget being ecstatic one year at girl's camp when Hailey found me and told me one of the girls in her group was Korean. Not only did she have her Korean background, but Hailey informed me she had just moved to the States from South Korea and barely spoke any English. This girl was in a different section of the camp from me, but I knew right away I was meant to be friends with her. I left my group and went to meet her.

When I found her, she was sitting alone with sadness in her eyes. I hesitated to talk with her because she didn't look like she wanted to be approached. I tried introducing myself in English, and we were able to communicate a little to each other. I decided it was time to get out of my comfort zone and just attempt some of the language I had been studying—hoping I wouldn't completely butcher it. As soon as I introduced myself in Korean, this sweet girl lit up. She told me her name was Risu, and I expressed to her my love for all things Korean and my obsession for Korean boy bands. I felt the energy shift between us, and we became very comfortable with each other very fast. The time came for me to head back to my group in the camp, and as I walked back, I couldn't wait to get to know more about Risu.

My leaders didn't seem to share the same love and concern as I did however. I started to have to sneak away from my level to befriend Risu, and the more I learned about her situation, the more I felt drawn to be her friend. I learned she had just moved to North Carolina the week before coming to girl's camp. She wasn't a member of our church, but she had an uncle who used to be a member, and he thought it might be a good way for Risu to be immersed in English. She was terrified to be there and couldn't understand much of what was going on.

There was one day when my level had free time, so I went up to Risu's group and sat with her and made bracelets with her and her group. We walked around the campground trying to communicate in broken English and Korean and using a lot of charades, and we had a great time. Dinner came around, and I headed back to my camp. As we were eating, Risu came running up to me looking concerned. I found out she had lost her bracelet somewhere between our two campgrounds, and she was pretty sad about it. I quickly left the table to help her search before the sun went down.

It took us twenty minutes or so, but we finally found it smashed on the trail. She shrugged her shoulders and I put my arm around her, and we both smiled. I loved my new friend, and I was so happy she was at Young Women camp. I wondered if she could still feel the Spirit during our devotionals or activities, despite not knowing the language. We went our separate ways, and I returned to my camp as they were cleaning dinner up.

My leaders were livid. They had thrown out my food and sat me down for a lecture about sticking with the plan and my level of girls, and then they made me clean up all the dishes. No matter how much I tried to reason with them, the situation, or explain how I felt like it was the right thing for me to go and look for Risu's bracelet with her, they wouldn't have it. It brought me to tears, bless my fragile young self, and I became really discouraged.

When I reflected on my experience that night, I remembered having feelings of hurt and confusion and not knowing what to do about the way my leaders had reacted. Very clearly in my mind a scripture came to me: "And the King shall answer and say unto them, Verily I say unto you, Inasmuch as ye have done it unto one of the least of these my brethren, ye have done it unto me" (Matthew 25:40). And immediately my heart was at peace.

It didn't matter what other people thought about me or what they knew about the situation. It was tough and disappointing that my church leaders were the ones who discouraged my interactions with the only girl there who wasn't even a member of the Church, but regardless, it didn't need to change what I knew to be right. I knew right then and there what the Lord would have done and what He expected from me.

I thought of the times in Christ's life when He associated with less popular crowds because He knew why He was there. He lived to uplift, minister, heal, serve, and be friends with others. In my mind that night, it was clear to me that the right thing was the unpopular thing. The right thing was the uncomfortable thing. The right thing was to forget protocol for a minute and cater to the needs of the individual.

The rest of camp I followed the Spirit, and I am so grateful that I did. Risu and I became great friends, and our friendship lasted throughout our time living in North Carolina. She blessed my life. I was able to meet her extended family, hear their incredible story, and learn more about their beautiful culture. I remember her family coming to our house on multiple occasions to teach us how to make Korean food. They made us art and books, and I learned so much from their family, and my interactions with them deeply enriched my life.

Being the only one can be difficult, but I promise that if you follow the voice and feelings in your head and heart to do good, you cannot go wrong. Those promptings come from God, and though it may be an uncomfortable situation at first, I have found that following through on promptings I receive from the Lord always leads to miracles. You can't go wrong for doing what you know is right. The Lord will bless you for having courage to stand up for what you believe in and what's important to you. Follow your heart, follow the Spirit, and, "Let your light so shine before men, that they may see your good works, and glorify your Father which is in heaven" (Matthew 5:16). I can assure you that following the will of the Lord and doing what He might do in the various situations you find yourself in will lead you to even greater blessings and a stronger testimony of His awareness of you.

As Thomas S. Monson so beautifully put, "May we maintain the courage to defy the consensus. May we ever choose the harder right instead of the easier wrong. As we contemplate the decisions we make in our lives each day—whether to make this choice or that choice—if we choose Christ, we will have made the correct choice."[1] I know that choosing Christ's way will bring you great joy in life. Being the only one will keep you from living a life of regret and will reassure you that you can be at peace because you did the right thing, especially if it was in the service of a fellow sister, and you have the Lord's approval.

NOTE

1. Thomas S. Monson, "Choices," *Ensign*, May 2016.

Chapter 11

SEEING WITH OUR HEARTS

{ Hailey }

Have you ever tried on a pair of someone else's glasses? No matter how cute they may look on your face, they're sure to bring on an immediate headache as your eyes try and fail to focus properly.

Mandi and I are both nearly blind bats, as we like to refer to ourselves, and have had many unfortunate experiences relating to our vision. If you wear contacts, you'll know what I'm talking about when I say that tearing, losing, or getting something in one of your contacts is the absolute worst! An unfortunate turn of events can force you to go through an entire day at school or work with only one contact in, throwing everything you do off-balance.

I had a friend in college place his contact lenses in a glass of water one night because he had no contact solution. He woke up in the morning and to his dismay, the cup was empty, his contacts gone! He found out that his roommate, who had been thirsty in the middle of the night, had found a conveniently placed glass of water on the bathroom counter and had guzzled it right down . . . along with his friend's contacts. They followed this story up for months with jokes about how the swallowed contacts allowed my friend to see what his roommate had eaten that day.

Thomas S. Monson shares a story to illustrate the need to correct our often-flawed perception of others:

> A young couple, Lisa and John, moved into a new neighborhood. One morning while they were eating breakfast, Lisa looked out the window and watched her next-door neighbor hanging out her wash.
>
> "That laundry's not clean!" Lisa exclaimed. "Our neighbor doesn't know how to get clothes clean!"
>
> John looked on but remained silent.
>
> Every time her neighbor would hang her wash to dry, Lisa would make the same comments.
>
> A few weeks later Lisa was surprised to glance out her window and see a nice, clean wash hanging in her neighbor's yard. She said to her husband, "Look, John—she's finally learned how to wash correctly! I wonder how she did it."
>
> John replied, "Well, dear, I have the answer for you. You'll be interested to know that I got up early this morning and washed our windows!"[1]

Viewing ourselves and others through our mortal eyes is like looking at our neighbors wash through our own dirty windows, wearing glasses with the wrong prescription, losing a contact lens, or putting on someone else's glasses. In order to bring our blurry eyesight up to twenty-twenty vision, we have to look through the eyes of our Savior.

He has perfect vision when it comes to how He views others because He loves, perceives, knows, and understands each of us perfectly. He sees our whole selves in the context of the big picture. Practicing seeing others and ourselves as the divine beings that we are allows us to walk God's higher path of love.

Recently as I was pondering how I could better live in harmony with some of my loved ones, a distinct impression from the Spirit came into my mind that said, *See them with your heart.*

As soon as I got home I pulled out my journal and wrote those words down: "See with your heart."

A flood of insights and ideas came as I contemplated what it meant to see with our hearts.

Seeing with just our eyes is viewing others and our circumstances with our limited, mortal perception. When I focus on another person without knowing their whole story or being able to see the whole picture, I tend to be more judgmental, unforgiving, harsh, critical, assuming, and impatient with their flaws and faults. Despite my knowledge that imperfection is an inherent part of the human condition, seeing with just my eyes tends to expect perfection in others and in myself.

Elder W. Craig Zwick, in a talk entitled "Lord, Wilt Thou Cause That My Eyes May Be Opened," calls this process *looking beyond what we see.* He explains:

> We can't fully understand the choices and psychological backgrounds of people in our world, church congregations, and even in our families, because we rarely have the whole picture of who they are. We must look past the easy assumptions and stereotypes and widen the tiny lens of our own experience.[2]

When our big family goes out together, we attract a lot of what we call "stare bears." One of us will jokingly say, "Do you ever feel like you're being watched?" causing the rest of us to look around and notice those who may appear to be watching us. It's impossible to know what others are thinking, but nobody likes to feel judged.

When we choose to see just with our eyes, as we often do, we focus on outward appearances. Seeing with our hearts is the better way because the Lord *knows* our hearts and the hearts of others. "For the Lord seeth not as man seeth; for man looketh on the outward appearance, but the Lord looketh on the heart" (1 Samuel 16:7).

I would add that seeing *ourselves* with our hearts allows us to feel God's love for us. Jesus Christ helps us practice patience and self-compassion around our own weaknesses and shortcomings, helping us grow in love and acceptance of ourselves, which creates space for us to embrace the imperfections of others. Our patience with our own faults and flaws is connected to our ability to have patience with the faults and flaws of others.

The next time I saw a particular person that I sometimes struggle to love, I decided I was going to try to put this into practice and ask God to help me see them with my heart.

I prayed before I had to face them that I would be helped to see them as a child of God, to catch a glimpse of what our Heavenly Father sees.

Though this person had not changed at all, my eyes and heart were opened to look beyond what I could see. I felt blessed with patience that made it so things that would have irritated me before went nearly (I'm human, okay?!) unnoticed. When this individual spoke, I felt capable of listening with an open heart, rather than adding additional meaning to their words and getting upset or bitter. God helped me to be generous in my acceptance of who they were in that moment instead of comparing them to who they "should be" and ideals they would probably never measure up to.

Because I was helped to see this person through God's eyes, I understood that what I knew of them was so miniscule in comparison to who they truly were. My small glimpse into their story was in no way an accurate summary of who they could become. It was like the Lord had washed the dirty windows of my heart and placed the contact lenses of His perfect love in my eyes, making it possible for me to see things differently. I felt like I was more in touch with my higher, divine, and best self. I felt empowered to act like the kind of person I wanted to be toward them.

Just as we have to continually keep the windows of our homes clean, seeing with our hearts is a practice, one that will continue over a lifetime. Big changes in our hearts rarely happen overnight, but this shift in perception gave me a jumpstart to acquiring love in a moment when I wasn't capable of mustering it up on my own.

So what makes this shift in perspective possible? What can help us have a lasting change in our state of being toward others?

The answer is charity.

"Charity is the pure love of Christ. It is the love that Christ has for the children of men and that the children of men should have for one another. It is the highest, noblest, and strongest kind of love and the most joyous to the soul."[3]

Seeing with our hearts sets us on the path to acquiring charity, the pure love of Christ, and allows God's love for us to flood our lives. Looking through the lens of charity opens our eyes and hearts to a new perspective: Christ's perspective, the only perfect way of viewing others and ourselves.

When I allow God to help me look beyond my limited knowledge and see things with an eternal perspective, it's easier to see people in a positive and accepting light. Seeing with our hearts invites us to be more generous, forgiving, gentle, curious rather than judgmental, and open to loving people just as they are.

Open your eyes. See with your heart.

{ Mandi }

My friends and family who know me well know I am full of opinions. And I'm not afraid to express them. All too often I find myself looking at others from the outside and forming an opinion of them based off little fact.

A few years ago, in one of my singles wards in Utah, I came across a girl named Michelle. Michelle had quite the personality. She was a sharp contrast to most of the girls in the ward—she had a short pixie-cut hairstyle, often wore business slacks to church, and would even sing in the tenor's section of the choir. She kept to herself and sat in the back corner of Sunday School and Relief Society alone, hardly ever looking up from whatever she was vigilantly scribbling in her notebook. When she did, it was usually to insert a corrective comment, or ask what I perceived to be an invasive question to whoever was teaching the lesson. She was blunt, she was different, and she intimidated me.

At first, I kept my distance from Michelle. I watched from my side of the room and often wondered where she was from and what she must be like outside of church, and in my mind I was convinced we were complete opposites.

One Sunday we had a lesson on feeling the Spirit more in our lives, and Michelle raised her hand halfway through the lesson. I held my breath for what was about to come. To my surprise, she spoke softly and humbly and shared a personal experience about her inner struggles to connect with the Lord, and she ended her statement with, "If anyone has any advice, I would really like to know."

For some reason, most likely because my heart was softened toward her, my view of her changed right then and there during that lesson. When I looked again at her, I saw a struggling daughter of God, who, like me, didn't have all the answers. I resolved to get to know her better.

The following Sundays after that, I sat next to Michelle in class. I realized her notebook she carried was full of beautiful drawings and calligraphy, and it became a quick conversation starter. I learned she loved English literature and had an appreciation for music and global art. The more I learned about Michelle, the more I realized just how similar we were. We were both passionate about cultures and food, and we began to bond over both outside of church. I found out she lived in the same apartment building as me. We began to visit each other weekly, and she added such fresh perspective to my life. I soon realized how intelligent and accomplished Michelle was, and I loved how unassuming she looked from the outside. Countless times she would show up at my door with food, books, notes, and movies that we had talked about weeks before, and she thought to bring to me when she came across them. She remembered the details in our conversations and was such a good friend to me. She still is.

Months later, I remember walking into that same Relief Society class and scanning the room for Michelle. When I spotted her, I wondered how I had never noticed her calm demeanor and soft smile before. When she made her comments in class, I realized their deeper meanings and the thought that she took to express what she was saying. Because I understood her better and had the privilege of spending time with her as a friend in my life, I couldn't believe I had previously seen her as anything different from the incredible individual that she was. I almost missed out on getting to know one of the most refreshing girls in our ward, just because I couldn't get past what my eyes could see. Michelle was a breath of fresh air in my life, and she still is for me. Her spunk and eccentricity taught me so many new things and gave me confidence when I was around her to be nothing but myself. I pull strength from her example and appreciated her rawness and genuine care.

Now when I come across individuals who I'm not sure about from a distance, I try to first get to know what's inside them and what makes them who they are. I have found in doing so that I always seem to find many things in common, and my love for that person grows. Seeing people for who they are inside, for the goodness of their hearts, will help us create and maintain strong bonds with them. It eliminates the need for judgment and has the power to become a great strength to your personal life. Seek first to dig deeper in getting to know what's inside, and I know you will find that it is possible to come to love and understand women of all types and personalities. They may even become some of your greatest friends and biggest blessings.

NOTES

1. Thomas S. Monson, "Charity Never Faileth," *Ensign*, Nov. 2010.
2. W. Craig Zwick, "Lord, Wilt Thou Cause That My Eyes May Be Opened," *Ensign*, Nov. 2017, 97.
3. "Charity," Gospel Topics, topics.lds.org.

Chapter 12

MAKING IT COUNT, MAKING IT KIND

{ Hailey }

When I was in fifth grade, a few girls in my class passed around a paper with a drawing and some unkind words about another one of our classmates who wasn't very well liked. The paper was slid to me, and I quietly laughed at what had already been said about her and, I'm ashamed to admit, added something to it myself. I was definitely not seeing this girl with my heart!

When another one of my friends got the paper, she stood up and tossed it in the recycling bin before it could reach the desk of its subject. A little while later, our student teacher called several of us out into the hallway, where the girl we'd been mocking stood crying and upset. The teacher held up our paper in her hands and asked us to explain ourselves.

I was mortified. I didn't think anyone else was going to see it, let alone the girl we'd been talking about. Although what was said about her may have been true, it didn't make it right for us to talk about her behind her back. Our teacher had each of us apologize for our unkindness, and I felt so sheepish as I told her I was sorry for what I had done.

The words we speak and the things we say to and about each other matter. They matter a lot.

Our mom made up a little song she used to sing to us as kids that said, "We build each other by saying nice things. Building blocks, building blocks." Of course, when we were older and wanted to be super annoying, we'd repeat it back to her and say, "We build each other by saying *mean* things." To this day I still remember that little phrase, and no matter how hard it may be sometimes to hold my tongue, I know how unkind or untrue words can really tear someone else down.

Though I'm pretty soft spoken most of the time, when I'm upset I have a hard time controlling my temper, and especially the words that I speak. During a recent rough patch in our sibling relationships, my mom gave me a book to read called *Without Offense: The Art of Giving and Receiving Criticism* by Dr. John L. Lund.

I was totally offended.

Just kidding. But seriously, nobody wants to be told that they need to work on not offending others or being offended!

As I read this book it became clear to me that I had a habit of speaking what I saw as the truth without taking into account how my words might make another other person feel. Using the excuse that we're "saying it like it is" to justify saying something unkind or insensitive is not the best way to speak to and about each other. There is a better way.

Dr. Lund says, "There is no such thing as constructive criticism. To construct is to build, to edify, or to put together. To criticize is to tear down, to find fault, to condemn. The thought of criticism as being constructive is absurd."[1]

Sister, there is a higher way we can speak about and to others. Learning this motivated me to change! I wanted to try to improve the way I spoke not only to my siblings but also to my parents, my husband, and even to myself. I also didn't want to fall into the trap of insecurity, which often leads me to speaking unkindly about other women. I came up with a mantra that I repeat to myself often that has helped me become more mindful and slower to speak: "Make it count. Make it kind."

Make your words count. Make them kind.

Our family has often been the subject of what I'm sure the strangers who write mean, hateful, and unkind comments on our videos and posts would call "constructive criticism." I used to read the comments on our content, thinking it was necessary for us to be responsive and interactive with everybody online. The sad thing is, it didn't matter how many nice comments we received; the only ones I seemed to remember were the hateful and rude ones!

Another observation I've made over the years is that most often, it's other girls who write the most ruthless comments. I can honestly say that I don't know anyone in my life who would write a spiteful or mean comment on another person's post, which leads me to believe that the girls or women who are engaging in that kind of anonymous behavior must be incredibly lonely, unhappy, and insecure with themselves, and have probably forgotten who they truly are.

In the spirit of finding the humor in life, we try to laugh off the mean comments we receive. One of our favorites was a comment about the size of our teeth: "Who let the horses out of the barn?" someone wrote. We still laugh about that one! When we were teenagers hoping to land a record deal, we traveled to LA to play showcases for several major labels and managers. I'll never forget a response we got from someone who was managing a very successful boy band at the time: "Great potential with their music, but they're not very good looking girls," he wrote to our mutual contact.

We could usually laugh together at the ridiculous things people said, but sometimes comments would hit a little too close to home and I would start feeling offended or discouraged. My dad reminded me of a piece of advice offered to Dieter F. Uchtdorf that led me to shift my perspective on the comments we receive. When Elder Uchtdorf was called as General Authority, he was traveling on an assignment with President James E. Faust, then a member of the First Presidency. President Faust counseled him:

"The members of the Church are gracious to the General Authorities. They will treat you kindly and say nice things about you." Then he briefly paused and said, "Dieter, always be thankful for this, but don't you ever inhale it."[2]

Dad reminded me of this story and gave me that same counsel. "No matter what people may say about you, whether it's good or bad," he said, "don't inhale it."

I wish I'd had this piece of advice in my arsenal in high school. "Don't inhale" means you don't have to absorb what people say about you or accept it as truth. For me, that means I choose to leave the opinions of unhappy strangers to stay floating around the internet rather than in my head.

For you it might mean something different, like choosing not to inhale the taunting and teasing of a sibling or bully or the discouraging comment given to you by a grumpy teacher, coach, or professional who doesn't see you for who you truly are. There's only one opinion of you that truly matters, and that is God's. You are His child. He knows you better than you even know yourself. He loves you infinitely.

When you ground yourself in what He thinks of you, you can allow any praise or criticism the world offers to float right by you without believing any of it as definite truth, letting it make you arrogant, or allowing it to weigh you down.

Rumi is attributed with giving three guidelines to govern our speech, which I have found very helpful: "Before you speak, let your words pass through three gates: Is it true? Is it necessary? Is it kind?"[3]

Imagine if, instead of bullying, name-calling, teasing, criticizing, gossiping, and trolling, more people started checking themselves with those three questions before they spoke unkindly, wrote a nasty comment on a stranger's post, or engaged in a hurtful conversation behind someone else's back. We would have fewer issues with self-esteem, depression, and even perfectionism. We would feel more love, acceptance, kindness, and unity among women in our families, friend groups, and the strangers we interact with at work, at church, or online.

Have you ever been around somebody who is constantly tearing others down? We've probably all had friends who can always find something to criticize in everyone and their grandma, as well as other friends who seem to be bonded only because they have a common dislike for someone else. One truth I know from experience is that those "friends" who talk badly about others or try to get you to engage in gossip are guaranteed to be doing the same thing to you when your back is turned.

I try to be wary of those who are perpetually fault finding, knowing that when I'm not in the room they're probably whispering things about me to someone else.

If you have friends who are like this, you can set an example and teach them a better way by refusing to participate in gossip, true or untrue, about others. It takes courage to restrain yourself from joining in and instead choose to say something like, "I'm sorry to hear you've had that impression of them. That hasn't been my experience," or "Why don't you go talk to her alone about that instead of venting to me? I'm sure there's more to the story." Then you can choose not to pass on anything that was said to anyone else.

The story stops with you, sister.

I had an experience in college in which I learned the hard way to be careful of what I said about others, especially if it could be taken the wrong way.

I was talking with a close friend about a boy I'd been interested in, whom we'll call Joe for the sake of this story. My friend was trying to validate me after things hadn't worked out the way I'd hoped and said something like, "He must be crazy. How could he not like you?" I responded with what I thought was a funny comment that we laughed over, but it was something I would never have said to Joe's face.

Unfortunately a girl who conveniently happened to be friends with Joe's girlfriend at the time overheard us and found my comment offensive. A few days later I received some lovely texts from Joe, blaming me for some problems he and his girlfriend were having.

Though I was at first confused about what I had to do with anything, when he explained that he'd heard through the grapevine what I'd said about him, I felt horrible.

The girl who had decided to gossip about me really didn't know me and had judged me pretty harshly. But I realized how quickly one insensitive comment could be taken out of context and spread around by those who participate in gossip. I learned to be very careful not say anything that I didn't want to get back to someone else and to catch myself before speaking unkindly or sarcastically about others.

It's best to adopt Thumper's motto from the movie *Bambi*: "If you can't say something nice, don't say nothin' at all."[4]

For some reason, the hardest people to control our words about are often our family members or the people we live with at home, but aren't they the ones who could use the most love? Girl, you know I mutter my fair share of unsavory things about my sisters, brothers, parents, and roommates under my breath in moments of frustration, but I also know that as we desire to improve and pray for help from heaven, our natural tendencies to speak words of anger can soften.

Before you open your mouth, ask yourself if your words are intended to tear down or to build up. Is there a nicer way you can say something sensitive? Are you feeling inspired to speak out of love or anger? You may find it best to just bite your tongue. If a conversation starts getting heated and you don't trust yourself to say anything nice, keep your mouth shut, go on a walk or go somewhere you can be alone to clear your mind, say a prayer, and let the anger of the moment pass before engaging with that person again. I've seen how arguments and tension can be avoided when I take a deep breath, step back, leave the conversation if I have to, and take time to pray to ask God for help to formulate a response that aligns with the kind of relationship I *want* to have with my loved ones and friends.

It's usually better to just ignore the unkind things that may be said about you, but sometimes you have no choice but to confront the situation head on. If you must engage with someone who has said unkind or untrue things about you, remember, "A soft answer turneth away wrath: but grievous words stir up anger" (Proverbs 15:1). Choose always to give a soft answer; don't fight fire with fire. If you're not sure what to say, usually it's best to say nothing at all. Just let it go and move on.

If you have a sister or sister-friend who knows you like a sister, you know what it's like when you try to tell them a lie. It just doesn't work! I can specifically remember the last time I told a lie to our sister Allie, right to her face.

She looked me in the eye and said, "You just made that up. You're lying."

It was as if she could see into my soul! I wanted to shrink away and hide in the corner. Keeping our words honest and true helps us build trust in our relationships with each other.

When Mandi and I get into a little disagreement—or "tiff," as we call it—it usually takes a few minutes for us to cool down and see things clearly before we try to patch things up. Our recovery time from our disagreements has actually become pretty fast because we've had so much practice in resolving our arguments.

When we were growing up, Mandi wouldn't wait for us to come and apologize to her. She wanted to resolve things as quickly as possible and had no problem being the first one to admit fault and say she was sorry.

After our "tiffs" now, her apologies usually start with, "Hey man, we cool?" to which I respond, "Yeah, man, we cool."

Breaking the ice that way makes us laugh and cuts through the tension, allowing us to then talk through the nitty gritty stuff if we need to.

After an argument, no matter what was said or done, we still have the responsibility to do our part to restore peace. Instead of holding a grudge and letting things fester, I know that I can choose at any moment to let go of my pride, go knock on my sibling's or roommate's door, sit down on their bed, and put my arm around them and tell them I was sorry for what I'd said or done. If they were ready to hear it, we'd have a great moment of forgiveness and expressions of love for each other. If they were still stewing on things, they could come find me when they felt calm and know that I would be waiting with open arms.

There is nothing wrong with being the first one to apologize, even if you feel you've done nothing wrong, in order to bring peace back into your relationship. Learning how to apologize with sincerity and make restitution is a skill that will serve you in all of your current and future relationships down the road.

We're not a perfect family, by any means. Even though we don't live together anymore and see each other much less frequently, we still argue, disagree, and say unkind things to and about each other. But, I've seen my relationships improve as I give my siblings space to be themselves and make their own choices without criticizing them or comparing their decisions to what *I* would or wouldn't do!

While quality time together as a family is something we really value, it's been really awesome to discover that although we are daughters of the same parents here on earth, we are each unique daughters of our Heavenly Father. Though we share many things in common, we're very different from each other, and need space to discover and walk our own individual paths.

Over the past couple of years as I've embarked on my own path of personal growth and self-discovery and have practiced self-love and self-acceptance, guess what has happened? I've been able to tolerate and accept the differences in my sisters' personalities, choices, relationships, and career paths as a result. The more kind words I speak to and about myself, the easier it is to speak kind words to others.

In my experience, relationships are built over years, one kind word at a time and one positive interaction at a time. No matter how hard things might get or how difficult it may be to get along with someone you love, a roommate, or a friend, you can take things one interaction, one day, even one hour at time. Each time you're around that person (or group of people), try to make every word you say count, and make them kind. You might find that over time, your love and respect for each other will grow.

Recently, after a hard and long day when I was left feeling discouraged and inadequate, I decided to seek peace and reassurance by attending one of our beautiful temples. The holy temple is my favorite place to be! The inside of the temple looks and feels exactly how I imagine heaven to be: white, spotlessly clean and orderly, peaceful and quiet. Everyone is dressed head to toe in white, and bright sunlight streams in through the colorful stained-glass windows, making everything and everyone glow. It is absolutely heavenly!

After I had completed my service in the temple, an elderly sister I'd never met took both of my hands in hers, and with tears in her clear blue eyes, said to me, "You are so full of light."

I became overwhelmed with emotion. Squeezing her frail hands in mine, I responded, "So are you!"

In a moment when I was feeling inadequate and vulnerable, God sent a message of validation to me through words spoken by a stranger, to tell me that I was loved exactly when I needed to hear it. Her kind words counted for me more than she will ever know.

On another day in a different temple, a woman said to me, "You have the most beautiful spirit. I can feel it."

I felt like I was ten feet taller when I walked out of those doors and back into the world, all because of a few sweet words expressed by a stranger!

There is power in the words that we speak to change hearts, to heal, to uplift, to, edify, and to unite. I have felt it in my own life! You have that same power to lift another, expressing love for and confidence in a fellow sister who might be discouraged, heartbroken, uncertain, or alone. I pray that we will see the light in each other and have the courage to speak words of kindness.

Over time, the kind words we speak can help us build beautiful bonds of sisterhood and increase our capacity to love one another.

{ Mandi }

Being careful with my words is sometimes a struggle for me. Like Hailey, and all of us, I have had moments in my life where I have acted impulsively and said things I wish I could take back later. One of these experiences for me happened on a trip I took to Haiti with Lindsay and my dad. We were part of a group of volunteers working at an orphanage and helping teach in a small village. The experiences we had were incredible, and the people and kids we met were just as amazing.

While trying to be helpful and make the most of our experience, Lindsay and I made it a goal to do everything we could to connect with the Haitian people. We wanted to learn about their lives, goals, and dreams, and we hoped to connect with them on a personal level. We figured the rest of our group would want that as well, but to my surprise, there was one who did not. One of the kids of our trip leader came along to help. He wanted to be a policeman, and his top priority on our trip was our security— not necessarily connecting with the people.

Unfortunately, I did not have the patience I needed with him during our time in Haiti. I noticed all his cynical comments, and it drove me crazy that I hadn't seen him smile once the entire trip. I hated the way he would pull his hand away if a child ran up to hold it. I rolled my eyes at the earpiece and walkie-talkies equipment he used out in public and within the walls of the buildings we worked in. I cringed when he pushed a sweet man away from our van door when he came up to see if we wanted to look at his art. Every time he opened his mouth or moved a wrong muscle, I was there to criticize it. It was hard to concentrate on the good people around me and the new experiences I was having when all I cared about was doing something to put this boy in his place!

Almost every night I would spend more time talking to Lindsay and my dad about how annoyed I was with this boy's actions instead of how well I was doing with connecting with the Haitian people. On our final night at the orphanage, we gathered as a group to discuss the day's events and what we had learned. I thought for sure we would talk about the emotions we were all feeling—it was a rough day saying goodbye to the kids we had grown to love so much. Our leader turned the discussion over to her son. He opened his notebook, sighed, and stated, "It's important that you all follow exactly what I say at all times. We had a breach of security, and it could've been tragic." My fists clenched. This was one of the few times in my life I think I could've swung a punch. Thankfully I didn't, but I wasn't fast enough to stop my tongue. Right there in front of everyone, I let that boy have a piece of my mind.

I let every negative thought I had about him come out during that meeting, and both of us got pretty upset—so much so that he stood up in anger and stormed back inside the house before finishing his speech. It took me the rest of the night to calm down and let it go. That night, I had trouble sleeping. I was feeling emotional from our long day at the orphanage and from all the experiences and things we had seen since being in Haiti, and I was so upset with the actions of our leader's son. I realized while lying in my bed thinking that night, that I had almost allowed my negative feelings toward someone else dictate my own and ruin my entire trip.

The next morning, I still had been holding on to some of my pride, and the car trip to the village had some unspoken tension. We had to hike to the village, and it was a hot morning. Lindsay, my dad, and I sped past the group and made it to the village first.

We were immediately greeted by the most loving people with hugs and kisses, though we had never met them before.

When the rest of the group finally made it up, I watched in confusion as the chief leader excitedly ran and hugged the exhausted boy—grabbing his hand, smiling wide, and keeping her arm around him as they walked. How could she love this boy? I know she had to have noticed how he secluded himself from the group and didn't help with anything. There's no way she was oblivious to what I saw as his grumpy personality and annoying behavior. How was it possible that she had missed him and was happy to see him again? How could she even bring herself to hug him and show him love like that?

Later in the afternoon I stepped out of the schoolhouse to take a break and walk around. I ran into the chief as I was exploring, and she happily took my hand and led me up to her house. We arrived at this tiny cement home with a dirt floor and no windows. The entire house was smaller than my bedroom in my apartment back home, and all of her belongings were neatly stacked along the walls. She had a bed, a suitcase with some clothes, and a dresser with a small mirror placed on it. She extended her hand out, and I followed where she was pointing to the side wall, where a table, without even a chair, was set up.

She had her nice tablecloth spread out and a few dishes with food on them. She handed me a plate and motioned for me to eat. It was early in the afternoon, and as I looked at what she had prepared, my heart was touched. Chicken that I know she had to hike down the mountain and travel miles on foot to buy, prepare, and cook before we arrived in the morning; a plate of finely shredded vegetables that I know she had to shave each slice one by one with her knife to make; and a giant platter of fried plantains.

I didn't want to think about the resources she must've needed to provide that for us, and I felt so humbled to be on the receiving end of her gracious service and love. Looking around me, I noticed the boy enjoying the same meal I was, from the same selfless woman who extended her love equally to us. She gave us everything she had, even her food. It was in that moment that I realized I was doing things wrong. I realized that boy who was so hard to love still deserved to be loved. I realized it was not right for me to try to put him in his place.

The woman's selfless act of love and sacrifice opened my eyes and closed my big mouth. She changed how I looked at that boy and others that seemed difficult to love in my life at that time. She taught me the power of a kind gesture, a simple act of service; a kind word. The rest of our trip went a lot smoother as I tried to have a heart or understanding toward the boy in our group. I thought twice before judging, and I found my trip much more pleasant and the boy much less irritating.

All of God's children could use encouragement and love, whether we feel they deserve it or not. We can never go wrong as we interact with others in kindness. Speaking highly of others and finding ways to love and serve them are essential to our happiness. We can express our love through saying kind words and thinking twice before getting annoyed or upset with others. When I hesitate to think and speak positively about and to others, I remember the words of Camilla Kimball: "Never suppress a generous thought."[5]

I am reminded to always say and do things in love and kindness. If we suppress those ideas, we may never have the opportunity to build up another one of God's children. May we all remember to love the way the humble Haitian woman did. I am grateful she showed the same respect and love toward me, a stranger, so I could learn to extend that same love to everyone around me.

NOTES

1. John Lewis Lund, *Without Offense: The Art of Giving and Receiving Criticism* (Salt Lake City: Covenant Communications, 2004), 7.
2. Dieter F. Uchtdorf, "The Greatest among You," *Ensign*, May 2017, 80.
3. Tammy Letherer, "Use 'The 3 Gates of Speech' When Writing Memoir," *The Huffington Post*, Dec. 7, 2017, www.huffingtonpost. com/tammy-letherer/use-the-3-gates-of-speech_b_11915322.html?ncid =engmodushpmg00000003. Accessed April 26, 2018.
4. *Bambi*, directed by James Algar and Samuel Armstrong, Walt Disney Studios, 1942.
5. Bonnie D. Parkin, "Personal Ministry: Sacred and Precious" (Brigham Young University devotional, Feb. 13, 2007), 1, speeches.byu.edu.

Chapter 13

FORGIVENESS

{ Mandi }

In many different circumstances of our lives, we find ourselves interacting with women who come from different backgrounds, beliefs, and cultures. It can be difficult to know how to deal with differences like miscommunications, disagreements, arguments, and differences of opinion. Sometimes we may wonder what is the right way to go about our interactions with others when we were raised differently or think our way to be right. As with any of these differences, discord is not always avoidable, and we experience feelings of offense, hurt, pain, and injustice as we coexist with others.

Whether this is the case for you in your families, with your friends, or in many of your interactions in the work field, there is one principle that will transform how you see and connect with others: forgiveness. Every one of us could fill pages in our book of life of the many times we've experienced someone mistreating us or of times where other's words and actions left us hurt and offended. Often, we too could fill pages of the times when we have done the same to others, though we hope they will be forgotten. It usually seems each of us expects and pleads for mercy from others where we so easily fall short, but when the time comes for us to extend that same mercy to them, we hesitate to freely give. For some reason, it often looks like a better idea for us to hold onto a grudge, remain angry toward each other, and to wallow in self-justification for when it could be so simple to let go and be free of our hurt.

I remember as a young girl an experience I had in church after moving to North Carolina. I was around the age of twelve, a young woman in a new ward, having to make new friends and navigate new surroundings. I soon began associating with two girls in my class. At first they were kind to me, befriended me, and talked with me every week. We always wanted to hang out, sit next to each other, and be partnered up anytime we were together for church or group activities. Though these girls were slightly older than me, they always tried to include me, and I even remember them doing small acts of service that brought a smile to my face.

Then one day, something changed. I still don't know where the shift came from, or what the reasoning might have been for the change, but these two peers began treating me opposite of the kind way they had in the past. As a young girl, it became difficult for me to feel welcome in activities, not judged in church classes and meetings, and often I would come home crying or discouraged because of words or actions aimed toward me that had been meant to hurt and offend. I was confused, and things became even more lonely when my older sisters went off to college, and I had to attend church classes by myself. Things escalated as these girls influenced opinions and actions of their parents and my other church leaders to where at one point I was almost convinced in my teenage mind that they all had it out for me!

Looking back, I'm grateful things happened how they did. It helped me realize the importance of gaining a testimony of the gospel and a personal commitment to attend and learn with the hopes to gain a personal connection to my Savior, Jesus Christ. I couldn't go to church for my social life—I quickly learned that church was for my spiritual life. My parents were a huge strength to me as I dealt with bullying from both peers and adults and overcoming feelings of sadness. My mom often had to remind me (and all my siblings) to go to classes and activities with the purpose to look for someone who might be feeling a similar way and befriend them, so they wouldn't have to feel the same loneliness. I quickly found there almost always was someone in need of a friend, and I became close with girls younger than me that I otherwise wouldn't have. My dad helped me adapt a "kill them with kindness" motto that I still try to remember in moments when my frustration almost gets the best of me. This mindset has become a help in all my interactions with others—even with my family members.

If you find yourself in a position right now feeling wronged and with a need to extend forgiveness, maybe an old story will help you: It is one I hold dear that gives me great perspective and strength and a desire to work on reaching a point where I can let go of some of the bitterness I may be holding on to. It is found in the book of Genesis in the Holy Bible. It begins with a young boy named Joseph.

Joseph lived in the land of Canaan with his father and eleven brothers. Joseph's mother died when he was still a young boy during the birth of his youngest brother, Benjamin. With Joseph being one of the youngest in his family and the first child of his mother, Rachel, Joseph's father, Jacob, couldn't help but love and favor him. Many of us will recognize this biblical story of Joseph as the one with the coat of many colors. Jealous of Joseph, his older brethren mocked him and estranged themselves from him. What made them especially angry were the recurring dreams Joseph had wherein he became ruler over his brethren. They could not imagine their younger brother ever ruling over them, nor could they manage to listen to Joseph describe his dreams. One day, Joseph's father asked him to travel over forty-five miles to a city named Shechem to check on his brothers and bring word if they were all right. Joseph, only a teenager, willingly obeyed and left to check on his brothers. Once he arrived, he heard word they had continued even further, so he made an extra twelve-mile trek to Dothan, where he eventually found them. Seeing Joseph at a distance, his brothers' hate and malice consumed them, and they devised a plan to kill their younger brother.

Upon meeting his brothers, they tore the coat off Joseph and threw him into a dry pit. They sat and ate and contemplated what to do with their younger brother. In the middle of their conversing, they noticed a group of traveling Ishmaelites and justified their cruel act by concluding it would be better to sell him as a slave than to have his blood on their hands. They pulled him from the pit and sold him for twenty pieces of silver. Now having to live with their dark secret, the older brothers ripped up the beautiful coat of colors, dipped it in the blood of a goat, and presented it to their father. They lied to him that he had been killed by an animal along his journey. Jacob mourned for his son and for many years was inconsolable.

Joseph soon found himself a slave in Egypt. He was sold to Potiphar, an officer and captain of the guard of Pharaoh. Joseph faithfully worked on whatever task he was given. It was easy to see that the Lord was with Joseph in all he did. Potiphar trusted Joseph to be in charge of his entire household, and he indeed prospered. Joseph was well favored by both Potiphar and the Lord, but even after all his faithfulness and hard work, trial struck humble Joseph again. The wife of Potiphar lied to the entire household and her husband that Joseph had tried to wrong her, and Joseph was put in prison—the prison where the king's prisoners were kept.

Making the most of his situation, somehow Joseph befriended the keeper of the prison, who became so impressed with Joseph that he left him in charge over all the prisoners. While doing his duties looking after his fellow prisoners, Joseph met and served two servants of the king, a butler and a baker. Seeing both men looking sad one morning, loving Joseph inquired of them what was wrong. They replied they had both had dreams that had troubled them and left them wanting interpretation. Filled with the power of God, Joseph asked them to tell him their dreams for him to interpret. For the butler, Joseph explained he would be freed in three days and return to his position serving Pharaoh, and as for the baker, in three days he would be hung.

Just as Joseph said, within three days the butler was freed and the baker was killed. Upon the return of the butler to Pharaoh's service, Joseph requested he remember him and tell Pharaoh of his innocence, but the butler soon forgot, and Joseph patiently endured two more years in prison.

One fateful day, the butler learned Pharaoh had been troubled by two vivid dreams, none of which his wise men could interpret for him, and the butler remembered the young Hebrew boy in prison, who had interpreted his own dream and predicted his freedom. Joseph was immediately brought before Pharaoh, and again by the power of the Lord, he interpreted his dreams to mean Egypt would experience seven years of plenty followed by seven years of famine. He advised the king to save up grain and other food and instructed him on how to store it to prepare for the famine and provide for his people. Impressed by the spirit in Joseph, Pharaoh made Joseph a ruler over all of Egypt, second only to himself. Just as Joseph prophesied, seven years of plenty passed, and a great famine soon followed in the land. While everyone suffered, Egypt had food, and people came from all around to buy grain from Joseph to survive.

Hearing word that Egypt had food, Jacob urged his sons to travel down and buy grain, so the family could survive. Joseph's ten oldest brothers were sent, but the youngest, Benjamin, stayed back with his father. Jacob was still mourning the loss of Joseph, and he knew if anything were to happen to Benjamin, it would be the death of him. So onward they went to speak with the governor of Egypt (Joseph) to buy their food.

Entering the presence of Joseph, the ten brothers bowed themselves before him. I can only imagine the emotions Joseph felt as he immediately recognized his brothers and remembered the things he had dreamed of them as a young boy. They bowed before him, not one of them recognizing his face.

He roughly petitioned them why they had come all the way from the land of Canaan for food and accused them of being spies. Quickly and defensively, they explained that they had come to buy food in hopes to save their starving families. Joseph tested his brothers further, relating that if they truly were who they said they were, he would keep one brother in prison until they brought the youngest, Benjamin, to him. Joseph did not yet want his brothers to know who he was, so he spoke through an interpreter. His brothers did not know he could understand what they were saying to each other. At his request, his brothers turned to each other, in their own language expressing their guilt for what they had done to Joseph, and Reuben spoke up, "Spake I not unto you, saying, Do not sin against the child; and ye would not hear? Therefore, behold, also his blood is required" (Genesis 42:22).

The older brothers still carried heavy guilt for their sins, and knew if they brought Benjamin and something were to happen to him, their father would die of a broken heart. Hearing their words, Joseph left the room and wept. Filled with compassion and love difficult to comprehend, Joseph's forgiveness began to take place. In his wisdom, he thought of a plan, and when he returned to the room where his brethren were, he arrested Simeon in front of everyone. He charged them to return home and bring Benjamin to Egypt, or he would not release Simeon.

Not only did Joseph send each of them with provisions and food, but he stashed money in each brother's bag; which they found when they went to feed their donkeys. They thought perhaps it had been some mistake. Not wanting to take any chances, they convinced their father to allow them to bring Benjamin back to Egypt with double the money from their bags and many of their best fruits and herbs that they had left. Knowing they had to do so in order to save Simeon and the lives of their starving families, the brothers returned to Joseph a second time.

When Joseph saw them coming, he told his servants to prepare a feast so he could dine with them (which at the time was looked down upon for Egyptians and Hebrews to associate together), and he called for his brothers to eat with him. Fearful that Joseph might think they had stolen money from him and imprison them, the first thing they did was confess about the bags of money. Joseph put them at ease, "And he said, Peace be to you, fear not: your God, and the God of your father, hath given you treasure in your sacks: I had your money. And he brought Simeon out unto them" (Genesis 43:23).

When they all came in to eat with him, Joseph inquired of the old man, their father they had spoke of, and if he was well. They answered yes, and then Joseph's eyes fell on his youngest brother, Benjamin. "Is this your younger brother, of whom ye spake unto me? And he said, God be gracious unto thee, my son" (Genesis 43:29). And then without being able to help it, Joseph was filled with emotion and wanted to run and embrace his brother, but he turned away before his brothers could see his tears. He wept again in his chamber. He washed his face, composed himself, and returned again to his brothers to finish his plan.

At the feast, they ate and conversed together, and had a good time. When the morning came, Joseph sent the brothers away with more provisions and bags of corn and money. This time he had one of his servants put a silver cup in Benjamin's bag and gave instructions for his servants to wait until his brothers were a little ways out before arresting the brothers for stealing. The servants did as they were told, and each brother was told to empty their sacks to check who took the governor's goblet. Checking from oldest to youngest, the brothers watched in horror as the cup was found in Benjamin's sack. Arrested and brought back to Joseph's house, they fell his feet, and Judah began to beg for Joseph's understanding and forgiveness. In response, Joseph requested Benjamin stay and be his servant and the rest of the brothers leave. Terrified, Judah cried that he would not be able to live with himself if Benjamin was not permitted to return home to their father. Judah begged to be Joseph's servant in place of Benjamin, so the life of his brothers and sorrow of his father would not have to rest on his head.

Hearing the regret and panic in Judah's voice, Joseph could no longer hide who he was from his brothers. He cleared the room of everyone except his family, and audibly sobbed—so much so, that the entire house overheard him. No longer able to constrain himself, he asked if his father was still alive. None of his brothers answered a word. Joseph humbly responds, "Come near to me, I pray you. And they came near. And he said, I am Joseph your brother, whom ye sold into Egypt. Now therefore be not grieved, nor angry with yourselves, that ye sold me hither: for God did send me before you to preserve life" (Genesis 45:4–5).

How can a man who had to overcome so much look the very people who were his own brothers in the face and tell them to not be sad or angry at *themselves* because everything turned out okay in the end? How can he so easily express his acceptance that it was supposed to happen that way because of God's greater purpose?

This story brings me to tears as I think of the depth of the forgiveness Joseph was asked to extend, and I am left in awe at the choice Joseph made as he responded to his brothers after all that had transpired and years of neglect.

He would have been completely justified to take his brothers as prisoners, to sell them as slaves, refuse them food, or hold a grudge for the horrible things they had done to him. He could have sought revenge for the life he had to endure because of them. He could have chosen to hate them in return for their hatred and misdeeds. He could have had them and their families killed—he had the power and the means to do so, but Joseph showed no signs of hate. No judgment or disdain. No pride or display of power. Instead, from the moment he recognized their faces, he filled their bags with food and money and was consumed in love for his father and brother, so much so that it brought him to tears—that he could not even bear to be in their presence without weeping at the sight of them. What an example of love, compassion, and most of all, forgiveness.

Joseph's forgiveness does not end there: "And he fell upon his brother Benjamin's neck, and wept; and Benjamin wept upon his neck. Moreover he kissed all his brethren, and wept upon them: and after that his brethren talked with him" (Genesis 45:14–15). He lovingly embraced each of his brothers and then conversed with them after everything they did and after all that time.

Joseph was able to let things go. Shortly thereafter, he sent for his father and the entire family, including the wives and children of his brethren, and he proceeded to place them in the best part of the land to provide for all their needs. Whether they deserve it or not, Joseph ensured that his brothers and all their posterity prosper greatly.

Truly Joseph had a deep understanding of what it meant to forgive and let go of the wrongs of the past. His ability and willingness to do so inspires me, especially in those moments when I feel wronged or offended by others, which sometimes includes situations with my family members.

Though I never reencountered those two girls from my childhood, I am completely at peace with the entire experience. As I look back on it, I can see the blessings that came from relying on the Lord through the hurt and pain. I can see how my Heavenly Father blessed me with the greatest of friends in school and a closeness with my sisters that still carries us today. These blessings have enriched my life, and I cherish them, but the biggest blessing the Lord has extended to me from this experience has been His forgiveness.

There have been countless times where I have fallen short, said the wrong things, reacted unkindly, and done things I regret, and I am ashamed of it all. Yet God does not turn me away or hesitate and make me wait for feelings of peace when I ask for it. I am brought to my knees when I think of the times He has strengthened me and given me His own feelings of forgiveness when I could not muster them on my own. His grace is sufficient for you and me, and He makes up for where we fall short and where we are weak.

If it seems difficult, or even impossible, for you to forgive right now, call on the Lord. In time, He will help you reach a point where you no longer carry any hard feelings and where you will be able to look back and say to the very people you once were angry with, "Now therefore be not grieved, nor angry with yourselves, that ye sold me hither: for God did send me before you to preserve life" (Genesis 45:5) and realize everything you went through has prepared you for something else.

I think forgiveness is one of the hardest things we are asked to do in life, but God will not waste our time, trials, or tears. Everything truly will work together for your good, and we can learn to be okay with how things happen because they shape and change us and are the reasons why we can turn it around to help and understand others (see D&C 105:40). We will be required many times in our lives to extend forgiveness to the women around us at school, work, church, and even in our family relationships and friendships. If you haven't experienced it already, you will be sure to run into situations where forgiveness is required to right a wrong and move forward in love and understanding in order to be sister strong. Through the grace and love of God, we can find common ground with anyone who may have given us reason to be offended. Through Christ we can choose to forgive, and we can find healing in our relationships.

David E. Sorenson said:

> This is not to say that forgiveness is easy. When someone has hurt us or those we care about, that pain can almost be overwhelming. It can feel as if the pain or the injustice is the most important thing in the world and that we have no choice but to seek vengeance. But Christ, the Prince of Peace, teaches us a better way. It can be very difficult to forgive someone the harm they've done us, but when we do, we open ourselves up to a better future. No longer does someone else's wrongdoing control our course. When we forgive others, it frees us to choose how we will live our own lives. Forgiveness means that problems of the past no longer dictate our destinies, and we can focus on the future with God's love in our hearts.[1]

Joseph is a wonderful example of extending forgiveness to all who wronged him at different points in his life, but indeed the greatest example the world has of forgiveness is of our brother and Savior, Jesus Christ. He spent His life serving, loving, healing, and teaching all who were in need. He lived and died for us and lives even now with His hands extended to us to help lift us from the ground when we need it.

After suffering for our sins and being crucified, some of His final words on the cross were, "Father, forgive them; for they know not what they do" (Luke 23:34). He understands the emotions you feel and has already paid the price for the injustice you have and will encounter in this life. Turn to the Lord, and you will find peace and the power to forgive. You will find that He is the source of the forgiveness you seek to help you live in harmony in all your relationships. Jesus Christ is forever our greatest source of healing. Just like Joseph with his brothers, Christ makes it possible to let go of the past and knit our hearts back together in love. Forgiveness is key to developing strong bonds with all the women we encounter along our journey, and it will strengthen and deepen our love for every one of God's children.

NOTE

1. David E. Sorensen, "Forgiveness Will Change Bitterness to Love," *Ensign*, May 2003.

Chapter 14

LOVING OUR NEIGHBOR

{ Hailey }

Growing up, our grandma had a sign hanging in her house that would make me laugh every time I read it. It said:

"I can only please one person a day. Today is not your day, and tomorrow ain't lookin' too good either."

What a great reminder that God doesn't expect us to do everything for everyone every single day. His way is much simpler!

God asks us to start where we are, to start small, and to take care of each other one by one, as Jesus Christ did. As we strive to do this, He steps in and makes us capable of doing more than we could ever imagine was possible. Just as Christ "went about doing good" (Acts 10:38), I believe the key to increasing our capacity to love others is to simply serve them.

I've started praying for inspiration to know of just one person I can serve each day. As I've acted on the promptings that have come into my mind on a daily basis, I've noticed I've become more sensitive to the needs of those around me. Most often, the Lord doesn't ask me to perform grand acts of service. Most days, I feel impressed to simply call, text, or stop by and visit someone who might need a friend. Serving just one person each day in a small way has completely changed how I think about my time. People are now my top priority, and serving someone is always the most fulfilling and best part of my day!

A few years ago I was shown a simple act of kindness that had a great impact on me. While I was in school, I worked multiple minimum wage jobs at once so I could pay for tuition, textbooks, and rent, but I never felt like I could keep up with all of my expenses. I probably have lasting internal damage from all the of late-night ramen noodles I downed during those years.

Eating healthy feels almost impossible when you're barely making rent every month, but I remember one week after getting paid I decided to stock up at the grocery store to try to take better care of myself.

I loaded up the checkout line with all of my groceries, and as you fellow independent grocery shoppers know, once your mama stops paying for every little thing you want to eat, things can add up really quickly. When I went to swipe my card to pay, to my horror my card was declined.

It made no sense. I had just gotten my paycheck and knew I had enough to cover my purchase. I was *that* girl holding up the line while trying desperately to get my card to work. After a few attempts, I heard the person behind me say, "Let me pay for those."

I turned around and recognized him as a fellow student, someone I'd seen on campus but didn't know well. I tried to explain that I didn't know why my card wasn't working, but he didn't bother to hear me out. He stepped in front of me and handed the cashier his card, taking care of my embarrassing and unfortunate situation quickly and without drawing attention to himself.

Knowing that we were both in the same boat, two young college students just trying to make ends meet, made his small effort feel like a huge sacrifice to me. I was so grateful! Because of his example, I now don't hesitate if someone in front of me is in the same situation at the grocery store or a restaurant. I love how it feels to pay it forward because I've been in their shoes before.

For a long time, I believed that in order to make a difference I needed to offer some kind of profound, life-changing service to people who were suffering in ways that I would never fully understand. Bonnie L. Oscarson, a previous leader of the Young Women organization said: "We are touched when we see the suffering and great needs of those halfway around the world, but we may fail to see there is a person who needs our friendship sitting right next to us in class."[1]

Though my family has had incredible experiences traveling to far places to give meaningful service, I can agree with Bonnie Oscarson's observation. We don't have to look very far to discover those who might need a kind word, a friend, or a listening ear.

Matthew 22:37–39 reads: "Jesus said unto him, Thou shalt love the Lord thy God with all thy heart, and with all thy soul, and with all thy mind. This is the first and great commandment. And the second is like unto it, Thou shalt love thy neighbour as thyself."

Everyone is our neighbor, but sometimes I think we forget that it is our closest neighbors, friends, and family members who may be the most in need of the service only we can give them.

Sister Oscarson continues, "What good does it do to save the world if we neglect the needs of those closest to us and those whom we love the most? How much value is there in fixing the world if the people around us are falling apart and we don't notice? Heavenly Father may have placed those who need us closest to us, knowing that we are best suited to meet their needs."

I'll never forget an experience I had on my sixteenth birthday where I was on the receiving end of service given by two young women who lived in our neighborhood. We had just moved across the country from our home in North Carolina to California to pursue our music career, and, per usual, my birthday happened to fall on my first day at my new high school. I was already nervous about trying to make friends and starting over at a new school and felt worried that what was supposed to be a special milestone birthday would turn out to be anti-climactic, as I was once again the new girl.

I can best sum up my first day of my junior year in two words: Mia Thermopolis. It was truly the most unfortunate royal nightmare of a day!

No one tried to talk to me or was friendly. I went from class to class without a soul offering me a seat next to them or an encouraging smile. I felt overwhelmed and totally invisible.

Later on in the semester, someone *actually* sat on me while I was enjoying some sunshine in the courtyard. All I got was a, "Oh sorry, I didn't see you there." Hence the *Princess Diaries* reference.

My first day was so rough that when I came home from school I went straight to my room and cried. Woe was me! Not quite the sweet sixteen I had hoped for!

I hadn't been home long when there was a knock at the door. I was surprised to see two girls from our new church youth group standing on the porch with a birthday cake they'd baked for me. They didn't care that I was new, or that I went to a different high school. They had known it was my birthday and took the time to make me feel noticed and cared for.

My feelings of insignificance were gone as I hugged those two sweet girls who thought to take care of their neighbor: me!

Little did they know how much that gesture meant to me, and still does.

Being new can be so hard. We've been there. But because my sisters and I have been "the new girls" and felt alone so many times, I think we've developed sensitivity for other girls who may be new, excluded, different, or lonely. This empathy has helped us have the courage to reach out when we could choose to stay comfortably in our own group of friends and ignore them. Instead we try to get out of our comfort zones, walk up, introduce ourselves, and invite them to join us.

Even now, I feel those same insecurities about being new. Like me, you're probably going to be new or feel lonely many times throughout your life, and choosing to turn outward instead of inward really is the best way to open yourself up to making friends and finding opportunities to serve.

When I found myself in a situation where I was one of thousands who had moved into a new community, I started to feel invisible when my efforts to connect and get involved seemed to go unnoticed. I tried to sit by someone new every Sunday at church to try to get to know people and was disappointed when many of those same women I'd chatted with would walk right by me the next week and act like we'd never met.

I became frustrated and started to feel sorry for myself. I got tired of always having to be the one to turn to the girl next to me and strike up a conversation and wondered why no one bothered to try to be friendly to me. Was there something about my approach that wasn't likeable?

I started praying for a friend. All I wanted was just one friend so I wouldn't have to feel alone.

The Lord used my loneliness to teach me a valuable lesson. While I was sitting in church one Sunday, surrounded by these women who were my neighbors, our teacher shared a scripture that spoke to my spirit and helped me see those around me in a fresh, different way.

Mark 10:45 reads, "For even the son of man came not to be ministered unto, but to minister, and to give his life as a ransom for many."

The Spirit touched my heart, and I felt like God was speaking directly to me! It was almost like I was hearing Him say, *Even my perfect Son, Jesus Christ, who was the most kind, wonderful, loving, friendly person who has ever lived knows what it's like to feel lonely. He was rejected, despised of men, and hated. He was betrayed by His friends. But He knew His mission. His purpose was to serve others, and He did it without expecting anything in return.*

I knew in that moment that if I wanted to follow in the footsteps of my Savior, then I needed to stop worrying about whether or not I was being "ministered unto," and I instead needed to forget about myself and focus on ministering to those around me. I wrote the following in my journal about this experience:

"What a powerful lesson I was taught about selflessness and knowing that, like Christ, I'm also not here to be liked or befriended or served, but to love, befriend, and serve others."

My prayers started to change. I started asking my Heavenly Father for opportunities to serve so I could grow in my love for the women around me. Whether I felt liked or accepted stopped mattering to me.

As I got to know a few sisters better, I was surprised to learn that most of us felt the exact same way: lonely, invisible, ignored, and friendless.

How was this possible? If all of us wanted to be friends, why was no one reaching out to each other and being friendly?

I think it's because most of us, myself included, were turning inward and dwelling on our own problems, waiting for someone else to make the first move instead of being the brave one to step out and be kind.

It takes courage to admit that we're not perfect, that we need friends, or that we feel alone. It's an act of bravery to choose to forget about ourselves or whether people will like us or not and to instead focus on doing the Lord's work by lifting others. But it's only through these moments of vulnerability that we're able to forge meaningful connections with each other.

A little while later, I was asked to serve in a capacity that allowed me to get to know other women by serving their children. Those efforts to serve in the Lord's way alongside my spiritual sisters helped me feel more connected than just trying in my limited, human way to be a friendly and nice person. As I served families around me, my capacity to love and accept others grew, and I was better able to see them as God sees them. I developed friendships with strong women of great faith, women who are spiritual mentors and examples to me.

My Heavenly Father knew what I needed better than I did and is continually helping me grow through moments of loneliness, turning my sadness into joy and connection through service.

One of our greatest examples of service and selflessness is our dear friend Linda Jensen. On our family's first Sunday at church in a new town, Linda invited our mom to sit next to her, put her arm around her, and said, "We need you here." Our mom said that small gesture of love and acceptance is what helped her feel needed and included.

Mom later had the chance to serve in Relief Society with Linda, and they became fast friends. Linda made everyone feel like they were her favorite person in the world. She loved our family and not only became a dear friend to our mom but also a grandmotherly figure to all of us kids.

When Allie and I got our wisdom teeth out, Linda somehow remembered and showed up at our door that same afternoon with two big smoothies she had made for us. I remember being so touched by her kindness. Her thoughtfulness made our discomfort seem so much more bearable!

A few months later, Linda was diagnosed with terminal lung cancer. We were heartbroken. It didn't seem fair that someone who was so dynamic, so full of zest for life, so selfless and good would have to face something so painful and harrowing.

In the year after Linda's diagnosis, she became like a second mother to me.

I would take her to lunch or visit her house at least once a week and looked forward to being with her. She made me feel beautiful, treasured, and loved. As she started her chemo and radiation treatments, I watched her slowly grow more tired, and our trips out of the house became less frequent. I tried to serve her in the best ways that I could, but she would quickly change the subject when I'd try to ask her about herself, her treatments, and how she was feeling. "I'm just fine!" she'd say. "How are you, my dear?"

Sometimes I'd bring over my guitar and play her new songs I had written. She would close her eyes and smile as she listened. She loved our music and made me feel like I was the most talented person she knew.

Once the weather got warmer, we would sit outside on a big swing in her backyard and just talk and eat treats together. One day in the spring, she let me help her plant her flower garden in her backyard and taught me all about the flowers she loved so much.

I would go to see Linda hoping I could cheer her up and make her burden a little lighter and would leave feeling like my own burdens and problems had disappeared.

When I got engaged, Linda wanted to hear all about it and loved getting to know my soon-to-be husband. She came to my bridal shower and stayed as long as she could, cheerfully chatting away while her son sat outside in the car, ready to take her home as soon as the pain became too much for her.

Linda and her husband were there at my wedding, embracing us and crying with us and sharing that happy day with me even though she was so sick and weak. She truly was one of the most selflessly loving women I have ever known. I mattered to her and she loved me, and I knew it, not just because she would tell me, but through her actions.

Just before Christmas, I wrote in my journal:

We've had the chance to visit our dear Linda each week this past month, both in the hospital and in her home. She has exhausted all of her treatment options and was given just a few weeks to live during her hospital stay. She has really deteriorated; she's lost all her hair and her ability to do just about everything. She is still so cheerful and has so much faith!

A few days before Linda passed away, my mom, my sisters, and I went to her house and sang some of her favorite songs for her. I quote from another journal entry:

Yesterday as we sang songs about Christ, it invited the most beautiful, peaceful spirit into their home, and I was reminded of a scripture I had read this week:

"Inasmuch as ye have done it unto one of the least of these my brethren, ye have done it unto me" (Matthew 25:40).

I could feel the most tender love for Linda and for our Savior as we sat under the glow of her Christmas tree, knowing that our service to her was as if we were doing it for Him. I know that He is taking care of her, and that I have felt His love for me through her kindness toward me. As we love and serve others, they can feel of the love of our Savior, and that's how He connects us all to each other and to Him.

That was the last time that I saw Linda before she passed away. I will never forget that sweet feeling of overwhelming love from my Heavenly Father, for me and my own family and for Linda and her family. My sisters, my mom, and I were bound together in love as we served together. We knew that our small act of service performed for one of His daughters was indeed recognized by Him.

We were able to sing one of Linda's favorite songs, "Oceans (Where Feet May Fail)" by Hillsong United at her funeral service, a privileged experience that brought us closer to each other. It was the most beautiful funeral I have ever attended! I loved getting to learn more about the woman who had been an anchor and dear friend not only for me but for countless others she had loved and taken under her wing throughout her life. I was amazed that so many of us who knew her felt like they were the most important person to her. What a gift she gave us! On her funeral program was printed her life motto: "The only thing that really matters is our capacity to love."

Linda lived that principle with her whole heart, even through her most difficult season of life. I know from these experiences that service, both given and received, purifies our hearts and fills us with the Spirit and with the love of God, and that it is the key to growing in our capacity to love each other as our Heavenly Father and Jesus Christ love us.

NOTE

1. Bonnie L. Oscarson, "'The Needs before Us,'" *Ensign*, Nov. 2017, 25–27.

Chapter 15

HOPE IN CHRIST

{ Hailey }

When I moved to Hawaii for college, I was immediately embraced by my amazing roommate, Luisa. Luisa was from New Zealand, and though we couldn't be more different from each other in many ways, we immediately became fast friends. She referred to me as "sis" every time we were together, and I immediately felt comfortable and safe around her because of that simple term of endearment. She was the older sister I never had. I thought I was so special, I thought I really meant something to her to be considered her "sis."

As I spent more time with Luisa, I realized I wasn't the only one who was special to her, because she called literally everyone "sis." She saw every woman she met as her sister and treated them as such. As I made friends from all over the Polynesian islands, I realized nearly everyone called each other "bro" and "sis," even if you were only acquaintances. I absolutely loved it!

Because of Luisa's example, I adapted her expression and have since called everyone who is not my blood related sister "sis," even people I don't know well. It's part of my vocabulary now, and I love the feeling of connection it gives me to refer to another woman as my "sis." Because when it comes down to it, that's what we are.

Luisa has become one of my sisters. I treasure our sisterhood and value her example and presence in my life, just as I do my own sisters. We can all try a little harder to take care of our sisters, just like Luisa took care of me. Maybe you can start by making everybody around you your "sis."

We are all imperfect people living in an imperfect world, and we are challenged with disharmony, discord, and contention almost every day. If there is one thing that we hope you will remember from this book, it's that "with God all things are possible" (Matthew 19:26). There is no obstacle He cannot help you overcome, no gap that cannot be bridged by His power and love. Most importantly, because of Jesus Christ, there is always hope. No relationship is too far gone or too lost for Him to reach down into your life and help you repair it.

If you're not sure where to start on your journey to living in harmony with the women in your life, start with getting to know Him. He will guide your footsteps and, over time, work to piece together the things that have fallen apart. I am confident that with Christ on our side, we can truly enjoy each other in sisterhood. We can laugh together, cry together, eat delicious food together, and build each other up. We can help bear the heavy burdens that weigh us down, "succor the weak, lift up the hands which hang down, and strengthen the feeble knees" (D&C 81:5).

Marjorie Pay Hinckley said:

Sisters, we are all in this together. We need each other. Oh, how we need each other. Those of us who are old need you who are young. And, hopefully, you who are young need some of us who are old. It is a sociological fact that women need women. We need deep and satisfying and loyal friendships with each other. These friendships are a source of sustenance.

We need to renew our faith every day. We need to lock arms and help build the kingdom so that it will roll forth and fill the whole earth.[1]

Mandi and I have so many things in common and really are the best of friends. But even though we're singing this song of life together and trying to sing it in harmony, we have moments where one of us goes off key, brings the choir down a whole octave, or stumbles over her notes. And you know what? We're better off for it.

As sisters, we've had opportunities to try to see where we might be part of the problem. There's no way we could count how many times we've said, "I'm sorry." We are constantly asking for forgiveness and praying for help to forgive. We lean on our Heavenly Father and our Savior to help us remember who we are when we inevitably forget and to help us see the best in each other, to see with our hearts. Whether we want to admit it or not, we all take after our mama and become more like her every day.

Sisterhood's no joke! But we're all riding this roller-coaster together. It's in those imperfect moments when we mess up and make mistakes that we're able to learn and to see things more clearly. It's never too late to clear our throat, fix our eyes on Christ, and try singing that harmony part again. We're still singing. Nobody's getting voted off this show.

As sisters, we're really good at sharing. We've used each other's perfume and toothbrushes (sorry, Mandi). We've accidentally crushed on the same boys. We've shared bedrooms and entire plates of cookies, and we've shared microphones. We've shared the spotlight, and we've shared the stage. But most importantly, we've shared the best and the worst parts of sisterhood with each other, and I would choose that over going solo any day.

We hope that you will lock arms and raise your voices with us in harmony because we need each other. Because of Jesus

Christ, we can live in harmony no matter how different we may be from each other. With Him as our advocate, mediator, and mentor, we know that we can forgive, develop charity, and change our very hearts and natures. With Jesus Christ, we can become sister strong.

NOTE

1. Marjorie Pay Hinckley and Virginia H. Pearce, *Glimpses into the Life and Heart of Marjorie Pay Hinckley* (Salt Lake City: Deseret Book, 1999), 254.

Acknowledgments

We would like to thank our sisters at Cedar Fort who helped make our dream of writing a book together possible! To Tracy, Briana, Misty, Allie, and Kaitlin for believing in our vision and for guiding us with your amazing ideas.

We'd also like to thank our amazing online family who has been with us on this journey over the past ten years. Thank you for making yet another dream of ours come true. We love our Gardinerds!

{ Mandi }

Mom and Dad, thank you for your unconditional love and support and for all your years of sacrifice. You have selflessly lived Christ-centered lives and shown me how to value family and relationships more than anyone else. I wouldn't be who I am without you, and I hope to become more like you. I love you so much!

Allie, Lindsay, Abby, Ben, Tim, and Lucy—you're my favorite people on the planet. Thank you for your funny personalities and all the good times that gave me something to write about. I couldn't picture life without a single one of you, and I just adore you! Thank you for being there for me through it all. I'm grateful our family is forever.

Thank you to Hailey, my partner in crime. I mean on this project. If I could be you, I probably would. You are a steady force, and I have looked up to you my entire life. Without fail you have showed me what it looks like to be an incredible friend and sister, and I'm so grateful for your encouragement and advice. Thank you for letting me join in on your brilliant ideas and inspired projects. I can't wait to see what's next!

Becca, CC, Jess, Aloha, Cambry, and Alexa: Thank you for your love and encouragement. Thank you for all the late-night conversations, for the FaceTime brainstorming sessions, and for being the greatest friends I could ever ask for. You inspire me. Thank you for all the chocolate and moral support and for helping me complete this book. Y'all give me life!

Thank you to Linda for being the most incredible woman I have ever met. Knowing you has blessed my life, and I always think of you. Thank you for your heart of gold and for letting me feel your love—though you are no longer with us. You were, are, and will always be an angel to me.

I am most grateful to my Heavenly Father, for being the source of all the incredible experiences and opportunities I have had in my life. I am so grateful You are the one in control. Thank You for life, love, happiness, my family, and for Your goodness.

My source of hope and joy comes from my Savior, Jesus Christ. You are my rock and foundation and guiding light through life. Because of Your love and sacrifice for me, I know anything is possible, and You will never fail me. Thank You for being the ultimate brother, friend, healer, and teacher. I know I can lean on You and turn to You always, and for that I am forever indebted and grateful.

{ Hailey }

Mom and Dad, who made me a sister. I'll forever be grateful for our two wonderful parents who raised us in a Christ-centered home. Thank you for your love, counsel, insight, and wisdom that has helped shape me in more ways than you'll ever know! I love you both so much.

Allie, Lindsay, Abby, Ben, Tim, and Lucy, who've loved me despite the fact that I'm their oldest and bossiest sister. You're each so precious to me, and I treasure our relationships with all my heart. We have many years ahead of us, and I can't wait to continue learning from you as we laugh and eat our way through life together.

Thank you to my little buddy, Mandi, my partner on this project. I learn so much from you by the way you love and treat everyone like family. You've always been wise beyond your years. Thank you for bringing harmony to the world and teaching me what it means to be sister strong.

To my best friend and sweet husband, Cayden; thank you for offering your cheerful optimism, advice, and faith in everything I do. I'm beyond blessed to have you by my side forever!

Thank you to all the women in my life who have set the example of true sisterhood for me. I look up to you and want to be as faithful and grounded in Christ as you are.

And of course, all praise goes to my loving Heavenly Father, who has blessed me with a forever family and with sisters to walk by my side. I want to spend every day of my life serving You.

Everything I am and every good thing I have has come because of my Savior, Jesus Christ. He is the way, the truth, and the light, and all things are made possible, including this book, because of Him.

About the Authors

Sibling harmony comes easily to this family of songwriting sisters. Hailey and Mandi Gardiner, the oldest and third children of eight, are singers and storytellers from Concord, North Carolina. For over ten years, they have performed together in their family band, called Gardiner Sisters. Alongside four other sisters, these independent artists have garnered over 90 million views on YouTube and 255 million streams on Spotify, and they have toured all across North America in a big family van.

In 2018, Gardiner Sisters released their first full-length album, *Covers Vol. I*, a collection of acoustic songs showcasing their signature complex harmonies and laid-back sound.

Gardiner Sisters' mission is to inspire and empower their peers to discover their identity as children of a loving God and to reach their divine potential. The family has navigated the entertainment industry, produced over one hundred songs, and run two YouTube channels and an inspirational blog, all while remaining rooted in their relationships, values, and faith. The unique experiences Hailey and Mandi share together, both as siblings and in their career as musicians, have inspired them to gather everyone into their family by creating positive and uplifting content and loving and embracing each other in a spirit of sisterhood.

You can stream music by the Gardiner Sisters on Spotify and find them on YouTube at www.youtube.com/gardinersisters.

{ Mandi }

Mandi Gardiner is a sister, chef, adventurer, singer, and pasta-eating machine. She hopes to one day finish her degree in English so she can write teen-fiction novels and children's books for the rest of her life. Whether it be through music, social media, or travel, Mandi searches for quality human connection and relationships with others. She loves picking up life tips and tricks that bring joy along the way! Sharing her life and heart online, Mandi writes about all things beautiful and soulful alongside her family on www.sistersandsage.com.

Scan to visit

www.sistersandsage.com

{ Hailey }

Hailey Gardiner, the oldest and bossiest child of eight, is a singer, songwriter, storyteller, and master at quoting movies. After living on the sunny beaches of Hawaii while earning her degree in international cultural studies, she now spends her time writing songs and stories and traveling with her darling husband. Hailey is passionate about helping others reach their creative potential and provides mentoring and resources for fellow musicians, writers, and creators at www.haileygardinermusic.com.

Scan to visit

www.haileygardinermusic.com